MW00579812

Briton Publishing LLC
1237 Glenwood Trail
Batavia, Ohio 45103
www.britonpublishing.com

ISBN:
978-1-0879-5722-7 Hardcover
978-1-7353-8344-6 Paperback

www.britonpublishing.com

CONSIDER YOUR ASS KISSED

BY

Ruta Lee

...and urged to do so by Texas PR maven Barry Rogers who insisted that my stories should be shared... and Judy Diamond, my Gal Friday, and Every day, who nudged me to the finish line.

Briton Publishing LLC
1237 Glenwood Trail
Batavia, Ohio 45103
www.britonpublishing.com

ISBN:
978-1-0879-5722-7 Hardcover
978-1-7353-8344-6 Paperback

Copyright©2020, Second Edition 2021

www.britonpublishing.com

Foreword

I met Ruta in 1975, when she joined me as co-hostess on the TV Game Show - High Rollers. She was already an established Hollywood figure who had worked with many of the major stars. I was still a neophyte. We worked together for two and a half years, and thru her and her work with *The Thalians* charity, which she chaired, she brought me into contact with many of those stars and helped make me a member of the larger show biz community also, a big plus for me and my career.

However, the biggest positive is that we have remained dear friends for 45 years --- so I know the stories she has to tell.

You'll love this!

Alex Trebek – *(July 22, 1940 – November 8, 2020)*

TABLE OF CONTENTS

Introduction

In the Driver's Seat

I find myself driving on a continuously intriguing road through life. I'm looking at the rearview mirror, appreciating the places that I've been, and the people who were there with me. I can see reflections of those I've lost, they're smiling at me, they're ok.

I can't look back too often, as I'm driving at a fairly high rate of speed into the future, and you never really know what's ahead. Occasionally I tap my brakes, being hesitant about that next turn, however, I never come to a full stop or go into reverse. Hell, I'm too curious about what's coming. As long as the engine's running, I keep rolling. Don't get me wrong. I go in for an occasional tune up, but that's ok.

I've enjoyed my past tremendously, and I also have a wonderful, anticipatory feeling, of, "Here we go!" It's always a little too busy to suit me. Maybe that's just part of what makes me tick and what keeps the juices going. I'm always extremely busy, in a rush; something always going on, someone always needs something.

My annual New Year's Resolution is that I'm going to slow down and not take on so much... really just kidding myself; I haven't slowed down my entire life.

While I've been in the driver's seat since childhood, I am also driven by the fact there's so much to do, and never enough time to do it. I know we only get so many days on this earth. The bible tells us that we could have one hundred and twenty years. Well, I want every single one of them! In fact, I talk to God about that every day. I say, "Listen here LADY..."

Ruta Lee

Chapter 1

How I Got Laid

on Hollywood Boulevard

Johnny Grant – Debbie Reynolds – Alex Trebek
– Leron Gubler – Oh Happy Day!

I was getting laid in wet cement with Tiger Woods' balls flying over my head! Ooops let me clarify that, I was getting my star on the Hollywood Walk of Fame in the prime location, at Grauman's Chinese Theater. Tiger was doing a golf promotion, same time, same place. About 1,500 of my friends, fans and press had gathered for the ceremony.

The city had made a mistake and issued permits for two events at the same time, same place. Tiger was hitting balls from in front of the Theatre, down to Highland Avenue. Don't you think he could've come over and said, "Hello" or "How are you?" He did not. Who knows? Maybe he thought that all the media and fans were his. Sorry Tiger, they were mine.

The day was so incredible. Legends like Debbie Reynolds and Mitzi Gaynor were there to lend their support along with so many other beautiful and celebrated people. I had done a lot of USO shows with Johnny Grant, honorary Mayor of Hollywood, who officiated over the ceremony. My alma mater Hollywood High School Band and drill team escorted my vintage '39 Cadillac Limousine, driven by owner Robert Ahmanson and son, Bill. (Wow... major philanthropist and businessman as my chauffeur.)

Buzz Aldrin - Mitzi Gaynor - Ruta
Over Buzz's shoulder Dick Van Patten and Joey
McIntyre

My friend of many years, Alex Trebek, one of
the funniest people on the planet, spoke. He said,
"Here's Ruta in front of Grauman's whereas my
star is way down Hollywood Boulevard, about two
miles, in front of an all-night porn shop with two
drunks lying in front of it. It's all about location, location,
location."

Everybody receiving a star on the walk of fame says, "This is a culmination, a dream come true, a wish fulfilled,"... and it was for me too. While basking in that delicious limelight, I couldn't help but reflect on my family whose sacrifices led to all of life's blessings that I now enjoyed.

My mother was the furthest thing from a show biz mother, yet this woman is responsible for everything that I am, have been or will become. I thank God every day, that not only did he give me that kind of mother, but that he let her live long enough to enjoy much of my success. "Momma Mary" was the eldest daughter in a family of eleven, peasant Lithuanians, working, tilling the soil, milking the cow, planting... Education was not a priority, subsistence was. Although mother only made it to the third grade, she was the smartest woman I've ever known. My father made it to the fourth grade but had a great deal of street smarts that helped carry him through life. Together they got us to California, but their path wasn't easy.

My mother and father met as teenagers. They married and determined that the best thing to do would be to leave Lithuania, come to come to America, where everybody believed the streets were paved with gold... Unfortunately, the immigration quotas to the U.S. were closed. They had their choice of Canada, Australia, Mexico or South America. Canada was right there, next door to the Unites States. In order to get into Canada my father had to sign a one-year contract to work in the wheat fields of Saskatchewan. My mother's family gave him what little money they had, to go there and take the job. He lived out his year contract and earned enough money to send for my mother and they then settled in Montreal, where there was a small but active Lithuanian community.

Mary and Joseph Kilmonis and the soon to be
Ruta Lee

Joseph and Mary Kilmonis started work as tailors for a Jewish clothing manufacturer, Mr. Simon. I will never forget that man. He really mentored my parents.

My mother and father worked incredibly hard doing piecework in his factory. They worked faster and more diligently than other employees. Mr. Simon would leave them the keys and say, "If you want to come in and do more, just lock up and turn out the lights." My parents respected him so much and the respect was mutual. Mr. Simon would include them in his family festivities. They kept in constant touch for many years. When he died, it was a sad day for my family.

My father went to work for another concern, eventually starting his own tailoring business. Whatever money he and my mother earned they saved and bought property. "Instead of paying rent, let's buy something, own it and rent to someone else." One of the buildings they bought had four flats. We lived in one. It was beautifully situated on the Boardwalk on the St. Lawrence River. While there, by their own hand, with very little outside help, they built a single-family dwelling next door. We were the envy of the neighborhood as Eastern Canada was mainly row houses. The river, the Boardwalk and the Natatorium were my playgrounds.

In a 6-day work week Sundays were really special, Mass first, then depending on the season, a picnic on the river, mushrooming in the mountains, berry picking or sleigh riding...always with a coterie of friends and much simple food and drink. A little schnapps never hurt.

When I was about three, my mother enrolled me in pre-school/kindergarten. The teacher, Mrs. Jackson, changed the course of our lives. She felt that I was a little different. Apparently, there was something a little more show-offish about me as she discovered in her children's productions. She's the one who told my mother

"Whatever it takes ... give her some dance and music lessons, she's different."

My First Communion-don't let that cherubic face fool you

My mother believing that I was Lithuania's answer to Shirley Temple put me into amateur shows, like Verdun's Bowl on the Boardwalk and the Roxy Theater downtown.

Holding on to my first prize earnings in show biz ($10)

I remember singing and tapping to Mexicali Rose in my little sparkly Lithuanian Russian costume that she made for me. I remember winning a prize watch and occasionally a few dollars. I would also appear in church and club plays. People took note and read about me in the Lithuanian Newspapers, so I was often invited to perform in other cities.

Wow, I'm talking about a little three, four or five year old kid ... not bad. My mother kept opening me up to any possibility. She'd just dream up routines and I'd do it; I must stress again that she was the furthest thing from a "show biz mother."

My immigrant mother didn't know anything about the New York theatre scene, which would have been the next logical step for her novice stage baby. But she did see movies and she knew they were made in Hollywood. My folks always wanted to get away from the harsh winters and live in sunny climes. Florida was a lot closer, but there was no "Hollywood" in Florida, at least not one that made movies. Momma Mary contacted the Lithuanian priest, who had started a parish in Los Angeles, which she supported, by sending a few dollars every once in a while.

This marvelous priest invited my parents to come out to his tiny little house/chapel on 3rd Street (the original Los Angeles St. Casimir's. He introduced them to a real estate agent, who showed them around and who took them to Earl Carroll's, then famous Hollywood supper club, which had a sign over the door that read: "Through these portals, pass the most beautiful girls in the world." The stage show was famous for its gorgeous women ... everything you've ever seen in the movies. My folks brought back a captivating souvenir program. It colored my life forever. I wanted to be one of those beautiful girls. Fat chance for this skinny, crooked toothed, wannabe.

This was 1947. You can imagine how wonderful Los Angeles was then. It was un-crowded, green, flowering and glorious. It was February, when we were up to our noses in snow in Montréal, but in LA, everything was blooming. They fell totally in love with California. Palms were waving hello. My mother cried all the way back to Montréal on the return train, seeing those tall, beautiful palms waving goodbye ... wondering if she would ever see this promised land again. Upon their return to Canada, they hand tailored a suit for the loving priest and sent it to LA. Sadly he died before he could enjoy it, but he was buried in it.

A short while after their visit to LA, a miracle happened. My parents got their quota number to come to the United States. I call it a miracle because at that time, all of the Lithuanian quotas were assigned to European displaced persons after World War II.

They liquidated the properties and most of our possessions. Within months we were on the road. I have such fond memories of our trip across the US. We stopped in New York and Washington. It was our first experience with American History and museums. It was thrilling to go to the Lincoln Memorial and think about how great this wonderful nation is. We drove to California on the famous Route 66 in a 47 Buick, which was the model with the long fish tail that everybody admired.

The new St. Casimir's Church in Los Feliz adjacent to Hollywood was a haven to us "greenhorns." We stayed at the church for a month until my folks could locate an apartment, find jobs and a school for me.

Our court apartment was on Fountain Avenue. I loved this location, because it was Bette Davis, who when asked how she succeeded in Hollywood, said, "I took Fountain" (an inside joke for movie people, as Fountain was the shortcut for anyone going to Columbia, RKO and Paramount Studios from Beverly Hills).

During the summer, I filled my days going to the movies. I was in heaven, as in Montreal children under 16 were not permitted into theaters. Fire regulations were in place because children had been trampled in a fire incident. I would fluff up a little bit and either walk to Hollywood or take the Sunset Blvd. bus. Hollywood had such beautiful theaters then, the Pantages, Warner Brothers, Paramount and Grauman's. They were all gorgeous and wonderful to walk into. I would walk Hollywood Boulevard thinking, "Somebody's going to discover me." Like everyone who comes to Hollywood thinks, 'I'm so talented, charming and adorable. I'm just going to stand here on the corner and smile at passers-by and someone is going to discover me." Those were the gentler days. Thank God, no one accosted me. No one discovered me either. I was still that skinny, crooked toothed wannabe.

Before we left Canada, mother heard of someone, who worked in the movie business, we should look up. He and his wife lived in an apartment at Hollywood and Vine. The husband was a bit player in the movies and the wife was a dancer. We went to see them and my family took them a bottle of booze as a, "Thank you for any advice you can give." They suggested that I join the Screen Children's Guild, which supposedly signed up children for the movies. Of course it was just another one of those "take your money and run" places.

Somewhere down the line, we found a woman who taught acting. She was an old character actress, Laura Kasley Brooks. Laura was big fat woman, 5'9 by 5'9 and jowly. She lived in a little apartment on Cherokee in the middle of Hollywood and I used to go over there after school and study for an hour every day.

My "Ms. Brooks" had several students. It was enough business income to keep her going. I was the only child actor. Laura would put together little shows of scenes from plays or movies. She'd rent the reception hall at the Hollywood Studio Club (which is where many young actresses like Marilyn Monroe and Linda Darnell resided). They had seriously strict rules there. You had to be in at a certain hour, no men and well regulated. Ms. Brooks would invite agents, casting directors, whoever in the biz she could muster, to attend our performances. Through one of these shows, I got my first agent, dear Lionel Thompson, a real gentleman. He and his father were old timey agents in Hollywood.

Through one of these showings, I was seen by the secretary to Ivan Kahn, then head of talent at 20th Century Fox. She told him about me and a meeting was arranged. There I was, all of thirteen maybe and he looked at me and saw something. I had teeth that were not perfect, and I was no beauty. He saw me as a young Anne Baxter. She was the queen of the lot when it came to dramatic work. He said, "Ok we're going to do a screen test." There were several coaches involved with new talent. One was Natasha Lytess (Marilyn Monroe's coach), another was Helena Sorrel. I will not speak ill of the dead.

I've never hated anybody in this world, but I've certainly learned since to immensely dislike Helena Sorrel.

She obviously took a dim view of the fact that I was brought in without her knowledge and approval. I remember her pale, pale face, and red, red lips and long, red nails. She would select a scene and have me learn it. i was best at drama and could make tears flow readily, rare for a youngster. She'd select fluffy little pieces. I'd go home, learn the scene word for word, practice and I'd come back in a week and she'd say, "Nah, I don't think we'd like that one dear. Let's do something else." This went on for months. I didn't recognize it then, but she was trying to sabotage me. My family wouldn't have recognized it either. The next thing I knew she wrote something silly for me.

Of course, Mr. Kahn never knew what was going on. Then came the screen test time. They fluffed me up in a pretty dress and the makeup department did my face and hair. This was the first time I wore false eyelashes. I thought they were the most beautiful things I'd ever seen. I did a scene, which was a wimpish-do-nothing little scene. It was about as impressive as a bowl of porridge. It showed none of my innate dramatic talent and ability. But I was too young and too stupid to know that I could and should have done better.

This was the beginning of the demise of the big studios. They started dropping all of their contract players. Of course I, who hadn't done anything, was the first to be dropped. That was my first experience at a big studio.

I owe a great debt of gratitude to Hollywood High. I had great fun getting there from our new Laurel Canyon home on the school bus everyday with David and Ricky Nelson. I also had some wonderful teachers. My favorite teacher was Helen Pointer, the modern dance teacher.

Hollywood High and my teachers gave me carte blanche to create shows. The auditorium is to this day, a wonderful theatre. It is often used as a venue for outside productions. I got to produce, write, create and choreograph Christmas shows, Easter shows and other seasonal programs. In fact, I got to do all kinds of shows.

My teachers were wonderful about allowing me out of classes for rehearsals ... classes I hated, like typing, which I failed four times. I was finally kicked out of that class and told, "Go take shop." I type now, but still in my own "hunt and peck way" ... works for me.

Hollywood High School – oh well...does anyone
like their graduation picture

My high school graduation was at the Hollywood Bowl. Some people that preceded me were Lana Turner, Alexis Smith and Carol Burnett. Several other famous attendees include Judy Garland, Charlene Tilton, John Ritter and Nanette Fabray, Rita Wilson, my good buddy Stefanie Powers and even the famous Judge Wapner. I still go to some class reunions, as Hollywood High remains highly important to me.

Harry Belafonte – Lena Horne – Sammy Davis
Jr. all became precious friends

During summer vacations from high school, I got a job as an usherette ... movie palaces had them in those days.

First I was in a theater way down the boulevard that played sort of artsy-fartsy things. I must have seen Stormy Weather, with Lena Horne, a hundred times. I knew all the songs. Who knew that in years to come, I would have her as a friend!

I stepped up a grade and got a job at Grauman's Chinese Theatre. It was just beautiful. The ticket booth was in the courtyard, amid all of the celebrity hand and footprints. The interior was red, black and gold, very oriental. Our uniform consisted of black pants along with red and gold Chinese Tunics. I was in my glory, standing at the top of the aisle, waiting to show people to their seats and then back to watch the movie screen queens.

I saw Betty Grable, June Haver, Ethel Merman, Mitzi Gaynor, those gorgeous women, starring in fabulous movie musicals and I'd stand there with my heart pounding, thinking, "One of these days I want to do that. I've just got do that."

Soon I got promoted to candy girl. Now math was never my long suit. Back in Montreal, when I was a little girl, I was held back a year in school, because I failed my math test by three points. While math was just never my strength, if you rustle a wad of bills in front of me, I'll tell exactly how much is there and how much you'll get, at six percent. I could deal with the candy counter because everything was ten, fifteen, twenty- five and fifty cents at most. I could deal with those increments easily, so I did very well. The candy counter was right next to the center aisle and I could stand there and watch movies until someone needed something. One night the cashier in the ticket booth got sick and I was told to fill in. Ticket prices then were $1.98, $2.35 ... stupid amounts that I didn't know how to deal with. There was a little machine that made change. The manager told me what to do: "You punch in the number of tickets at the price and punch in the amount you're given. The machine will give the right change."

Well, at the end of the evening, I was $40.00 short. I guess the machine made a mistake and gave away too much change... but I got fired. In tears, I said, "I didn't take the money and I'm sorry! One of these days I'll be back and maybe my footprints will be here in the courtyard of Grauman's Chinese Theatre!" Well, Lady Luck heard me. When I got my star on Hollywood Boulevard, I got the choicest location at Grauman's Chinese Theater ... guess where? ... right in front of the damn box office. One way or the other, I felt like that part of my life had come full circle.

Chapter 2

My First "Idyll" Wild Investment

When we lose something, God fills the void. Right around the time that I got fired from Grauman's Theatre, my best friend Carmen Hall encouraged me to audition for the chorus of *On The Town* at the Gallery Stage Theater. Some job I landed! This was like show business boot camp, hard work and no pay. Closing the first act was the *Times Square Ballet*. I was in a black beret, little black sweater, black mesh hose, very sexy, especially with the help of my incredibly well-padded strapless bra. As the lively number came to an end, I was lifted onto the shoulder of a big boy dancer, with my arms outstretched for a lovely finale. With the welcome applause, I heard lots of giggles.

As the lights dimmed, I looked down and realized in all the frantic dance movement, my bra had turned. I now had one tit coming out my side and one tit coming out my back. It was hysterical. Doing several shows at The Gallery Stage was a great training ground for me, as it was for other up and coming stars like Beverly Garland and Jeanne Cooper (Katherine Chancellor on The Young and The Restless).

One of the Gallery's associate producers worked with Burns and Allen, which was a huge television show at the time. He liked my work and got me cast. This was my first major show, on which I got screen credit and my SAG card. George remembered me all through the years. I was invited to their house on Maple Drive from time to time. When I started doing a lot of work for *The Thalians*, my lifetime charity, he would come to the events and sit at my table. This was long after Gracie had gone. He was a gent who always smiled, puffed his cigar and grunted, "Good girl. Good girl."

While working on Burns and Allen, I developed a huge a crush on Ralph Levy, director of the show. He took me out once to Chasens, a famous watering spot for stars and celebrities. I thought I'd died and gone to heaven. I remember wearing my felt poodle skirt. I just knew that he had to be smitten with me, if he took me out to dinner. I finally figured out I wasn't his type. Carmen's good friend, actor Paul Sand was his type. Oh well ... The Burns and Allen Show was the beginning of a lucrative television career. I'll always be grateful to George and Gracie for believing in me. I especially appreciate the director for putting up with my puppy love. But what the hell, I was his teenage "beard".

Not long after my television break, my high school dance teacher Helen Pointer invited me to a two-week dance symposium in Idyllwild - in the San Jacinto Mountains. "Come with me. This dance experience will be good for you!" Belaijus, a prominent Lithuanian folk dance choreographer, famous ballet master Eugene Loring, along with many outstanding dance pros, gave open-air classes at Isomata, which was part of the Arts department of USC. To this day Isomata is a wonderful school.

I went with her to spend a week or two. I can still smell the pine fragrance at the Atwater Kent Theater. It is a natural bowl with a plank floor stage. Felled logs made tiers of seating.

On this campus, one walks through the woods and finds many isolated studios, a cement slab, a wooden lean-to, and a music stand. Somebody might be practicing the piccolo, or the violin, or whatever. It is wonderful. I had been there once before with my Lithuanian folk-dance group. I remember how tough it was dancing at six or seven thousand feet. Doing the polka there . WHEW! You really had to have stamina.

While I was there I got a call from my agent, Lionel Thompson. He had gotten me an audition for a movie at MGM ... Seven Brides for Seven Brothers. I sped down the mountain to LA, picked up mom, then headed to MGM. Across the street from the casting office is, Saint Augustine Church. My mother went in, got down on her knees and prayed I would get the part. I went in, auditioned, and danced up a storm. I did a little ballet. Director Stanley Donen said, "Can you do a little Jazz?" I did that. "Can you do something ... kind of folksy?" Folksy to me is a Lithuanian polka. So, I polkaed up another storm. Whatever I did, it worked! I got the job... or maybe it was my mother's prayers.

After my Seven Brides audition, I drove back up to Idyllwild. Mr. Sarno, the history teacher from Hollywood High, invited Helen Pointer and me, to his mountain home for supper. Mr. Sarno, being Italian, of course had wine at the table. I was permitted to have a little because I was treated as an adult. After supper he took us to a place, the residents called Inspiration Point ... and inspiring it was. The stormy day brought out clouds that created a spectacular sunset. The residents would drive out daily to the Point - to watch the sun go down. The schoolteacher who taught crafts was part Indian. She would do wonderful chants out on the rocks as part of a ceremony. The beautiful, glorious sunset a sip of wine, being treated like an adult, brought me to copious tears. I never forgot Inspiration Point.

I started work on Seven Brides and when we finished shooting many months later, it was my earnings of $350.00 a week that put me into my first real estate venture. Carmen and I decided, 'We're going on a vacation and shopping for real estate!' We went back to Idyllwild. Here are these two teenage tootsies, walking into the real estate office saying, "Show us what property you have!" They showed us plenty of lots, but I couldn't take my mind off of Inspiration Point. They said, "Unavailable... all owned by Isomata personnel."

Fade out. Fade in. Six months later, the realtor called. One of the teachers who had the prime lot on Inspiration Point had to leave California. Her lot was for sale. I said, "Really? How much?"

He said, "$1,500!" That was a lot of money back in 1954. I said, "I'll take it!" Because I was under eighteen, I had to have my mother's name on the deed as well. I paid the $1,500 and about five years ago, I turned down $400,000 for the same lot. You can see why, to this day, I'm a firm believer of investing in real estate, not diamonds.

Chapter 3

My Lucky 7 Brides for Seven Brothers

"How do I get into show business? How do I do it?" Seasoned actors are always asked for advice by younger performers. There's no way you can tell anyone HOW! The star-making process is different now, different time, place ... all different. My universal rule - Get an education, so if you can't do what you love in show biz, you can feed yourself, while reaching for the stars. Being driven helps. Luck helps even more.

Seven Brides family...working with some of the
best dancers in the world was amazing

I think that most of my career has been serendipitous. I never chased roles. That's a fault. If I had, who knows what could have happened? It's not that I'm lazy. I work very hard when I'm working. I just don't work hard at getting the work. There were many social and charitable causes that grabbed my interests. My husband is the first to say that if I had devoted ten percent of the time to my career that I devote to my *do-good* activities, I could have told Barbra Streisand to get out of my way. He's right. It helps to be driven. I was just never driven with ambition.

I am blessed and proud that two of the movies I was in, *Witness for the Prosecution* and *Seven Brides for Seven Brothers,* are considered by critics, to be in the top one hundred movies ever made. In fact, *Seven Brides* launched my career. I'm forever grateful. When MGM decided to do this movie, originally called *The Sobbin Women* (a variation on *The Sabine Women*), they had no idea that this would become a Hollywood Classic. Director, Stanley Donen, producer, Jack Cummings, choreographer, Michael Kidd were responsible for its success. However, at that time, big MGM money was going into *Brigadoon*, starring Gene Kelly, Van Johnson and Cyd Charisse.

Our movie had Howard Keel, Jane Powell and a young Russ Tamblyn, but the rest of us were relatively unknown. B*rigadoon* was not the expected box office hit, while our movie performed beyond all expectation.

Making *Seven Brides* was hard work, but so worth it. This was the time of the six-day workweek .... two-day weekends didn't exist yet. We worked twelve-hour days and sometimes more. Dance rehearsals took at least six weeks on the musical numbers. The best dancers in America were in this movie. Our choreographer was the famous and fantastic Michael Kidd of Broadway's *Guys and Dolls, Can-Can,* etc... When we did the warmup/barre every morning, I thought, 'What the hell am I doing here? How did I rate being in the company of such greatness?'

I was paired with Matt Mattox, whom I had fallen madly in love with, when I saw him in *Carnival in Flanders,* a musical written by Meredith Willson. Matt did a pirate number in skintight leather pants and boots, brandishing a whip. Choreographer Jack Cole had created some of the most sensual movement and Matt performed it 150%. What a dancer and what a thrill for me to be paired with him.

Our director Stanley Donen was brilliant, and I worked for him again in *Funny Face* (Audrey Hepburn and Fred Astaire). He had a feel and an eye for theatricality that few could match. Early into 7 Brides' dance rehearsals with Michael Kidd, I had a couple of mishaps. Unfortunately, I sprained my ankle.

One of the boy dancers lifted me off a high riser and he didn't set me down gently. He sort of dropped me and my ankle went crunch. Of course, I was terrified that I was going to be replaced but they just let me sit there, foot in ice, to watch and learn. I didn't get put into as much choreography as I should have, but I didn't get fired either. The barn raising was the biggest number to set. It remains an iconic dance sequence, seen time after time worldwide.

The cast was awed when they finally let us on the sound stage to rehearse on the wooden plank floor. The soles of our shoes hadn't been rubberized yet. We were still breaking them in for filming. I did a big high kick and as I slid back, so did the shoes, I fell forward and smacked my head on the floor. I went out like a light.

There I was, spread eagle on the floor and I heard Michael Kidd say, "She's ok. She's ok. She just dropped a quarter between the planks and now she's looking for it." Of course I was in pain, but I couldn't stop laughing. Do you know how hard it is to laugh when your head hurts? That was the kind of guy Michael Kidd was. I adored him. Instead of saying three chassés to the right with a pique turn,(ballet talk) he'd say, "Three scrape alongs and one of those corkscrew jobs!"

I laughed and smiled my way through the whole yearlong period of production. It was a wonderful, WONDERFUL experience at MGM. The back lot was used for the woods. We thought we'd be sent to Utah to shoot the sleigh rides, but they used doubles there instead.

The avalanche close ups took place over Esther Williams swimming pool. Such is movie magic. These were the early days of Cinemascope. Not all the theaters were equipped for the process so each scene was shot twice. First for Cinemascope and second for Wide Screen.

Real life brides usually change their name after marriage. In this "movie bride's" case, it happened before.

As the studio became aware that they had a potential hit on their hands, the publicity department came around to all the girls and said, "We're sending you on personal appearance tours. Each girl will get a section of the country. I was assigned everything west of the Continental Divide. Before leaving on the tour, the P.R. people came to me and said, "You're never going to become a movie star with a name like Ruta Kilmonis." In high school, two years earlier, I had said to my homeroom teacher Mrs. Volmer, "I was born Ruta Maria Kilmonis. All my life someone had thought the "u" in Ruta was a misprint, so I grew up Rita, Rhoda or Rhonda... but mostly Ruth. "Please everybody refer to me as Ruta." That is exactly what I said to the publicity department. They said, "Let's lose Kilmonis." We kicked names around for several days.

Somebody finally said, "How about Ruta Lee?" That rang a bell! The diminutive of Ruta in Lithuanian, Russian, Polish, Yiddish.... or anything, is Rutaleh. I said, "Ok, let's go with it." Ruta Lee was born.

My portion of the tour was highly successful. We made headlines - and news stories, gleaning great press clippings, which made the studio happy. They had Ruta Lee floating down the Colorado river, Ruta Lee playing baseball with the boys in Portland, leaning on a cactus in Arizona, chewing tobacco with the farmers in the Imperial

Valley, in a bathing suit with an umbrella in downtown Salt Lake City - during a thunderstorm.

Verdun/Montreal a great homecoming

RUTA LEE did everything and anything to get newspaper space publicizing the movie.

This glorious educational tour for this young novice was extended and I covered all of Canada from coast to coast as well. Going back to my hometown of Montreal, as a starlet, was very exciting and my reception was amazing.

Finally ... the red-carpet premiere at the Egyptian Theater in Hollywood! When the cast credits ran, I gasped. After all of the P.R. campaigning, I was billed as Ruta Kilmonis. Clearly someone in charge of the cast list had not been informed of my name change.

So, now you know those folks in all the cities I visited, are saying, "Who the hell was that Ruta Lee, who said she was in the movie?" Ahhhh, but God works in mysterious ways and turned a booboo into a benefit. Years later, after my world-famous call to Khrushchev (more later), I was permitted to go to then closed Soviet Lithuania.

The Lithuanians were so proud that one of their own, Ruta Kilmonis was in one of the rare American films that they were permitted to see. They loved it and ran it endlessly. The next time you see it on television, you will note that I am still credited as Ruta Kilmonis and now you know why.

More recently, I happily presented an award to Russ Tamblyn from the *Professional Dancer's Society* headed by Joni Berry and Mitzi Gaynor. While speaking of his many credits, I recounted a story, which embarrasses Russ like crazy. So, I just love repeating it! During the many months of filming *Seven Brides*, we would go to the movies, or have a sandwich together, or just hang out on the set and laugh.

We were such young kids, and he was adorable. Rusty came into the studio makeup room one morning in a lather and growled, "Son of a bitch!" You have to remember that all of the brothers on *Seven Brides* were red heads. All the guys had long died red hair. When they dipped Rusty's hair, it came up a Lucille Ball orange. In those days, guys didn't have jeans. They wore chinos, khaki-colored pants. That's what he had on and a dark blue sweatshirt that had been washed so many times, that it was now pale lavender. I said, "What happened?"

He said, "Well I'll tell you what happened! I walked into a little café on Hollywood Boulevard. I wanted to get a pack of cigarettes. I had to go to the cashier at the end of the counter. As I walked by, some ladies sitting at the counter, turned, looked at me and tittered shyly." I thought, "Oh they are beginning to recognize me as a star because I've done a couple of movies." As I was leaving, I really smiled at them and winked. I then heard one say to the other, "See Mary, I told you she was a lesbian!"

That can happen to a cute, butch guy with flaming red hair in a purple shirt. I repeat that story at every opportunity. I told it at the Academy screening and at a beautiful retrospective at the Orpheum Theatre. It was exciting, because as the film ran, every number was applauded, just like live theater. Being with the cast, sharing and reflecting on this timeless movie for multi-generations is always rewarding.

I can tell aspiring newcomers *Seven Brides* taught me that technical ability is 10% of what you bring to a performance. If you can sell it, it doesn't matter what your feet are doing. It is all in the attitude. Whether you're dancing, singing, acting, whatever, SELL IT! Do it with all your heart, that's far more important than technique. Let me tell you, Ruta (Kilmonis) Lee has been *selling it* for a long time.

Chapter 4

Making the Cut

People in show business are always accused of having big egos and not being grounded. I don't think I've ever really bought into my own press. Maybe I did for a few minutes after Seven Brides, but I had friends around me who said, "Ruta, knock it off!"

Let's face it; this business is full of hard knocks that keep you humble and some that really keep you grounded. Subsequent to Seven Brides I did several films. The first was Anything Goes starring Bing Crosby, Mitzi Gaynor and Donald O'Connor all of whom later became good friends. No one recalls seeing me in that movie. Well, there's a reason. Many beautiful girls auditioned. I was hired to work in a big party sequence. It took about a week to shoot the scene. I was so thrilled, because I got to meet and work closely with Bing, Mitzi and Donald.

With great excitement, my family, friends and I went to the première. This was an unforgettable night for me because I lived through that horrendous experience of discovering that I was no longer in the movie.

The party sequence with me in it was gone! It was unimportant to the movement of the film, I guess. You can catch a couple of glimpses of me in a black slinky dress that I look divine in.

On the road to Thalians Bob – Dorothy –
Debbie – Bing - Ruta

But don't blink, or you'll miss me! This was my first experience ending up on the cutting room floor. I cried all the way home. Boy, that was ego bruising and grounding.

The bright side of this humbling story was getting to know Bing. He and I used to sit and talk on the set. He liked me and we stayed in touch over the years. In fact, he, Bob Hope and Dorothy Lamour were *The Thalians* Honorees (Hollywood for Mental Health) at an evening we called Road to Thalians. Lest I forget, in later years, Donald and Mitzi became friends and vital to my life ... and *The Thalians* as well.

Second film was Gaby, an MGM remake of Vivien Leigh's Waterloo Bridge. It was always exciting to go home to Metro. That's where I shot my episode of Twilight Zone, still aired every year. It was also where I first met Leslie Caron, who starred in Gaby. I played a dancer in her ballet company, French accent and all. Many years later, I did Funny Bones with her and Jerry Lewis ... shot in England. We have since of course visited with each other on a number of occasions. I see her when I'm in Paris, attended her Hollywood star ceremony and lunched with her when she was honored at the Professional Dancer's Society in Beverly Hills.

Seven Brides director, Stanley Donen hired me for Funny Face, starring Audrey Hepburn, Fred Astaire and Kay Thompson. I developed a lovely friendship with Fred on this movie. He watched out for me and often over the years sent me critique notes. Like an idiot, I didn't save any of them. Fred was reticent about mixing socially with people ... however he liked me, and I adored him.

His daughter Ava and I became good friends. She would ask Fred to come over for dinner. He would say, "Hmmm, I don't know." "Well, Daddy, Ruta's coming." "Hmmm, ok. What time?"

Fred Astaire – I never got to dance with this legend

Fred had a gentleness about him. He had a beautifully restrained way of working both as an actor and dancer. It looked like he could do so much more, but he just oozed his way into whatever he was doing. On the flip side, I'm bigger than life. It's just the way I am. Maybe Fred liked that. He was very sweet with me. Oh hell, if I'd played my cards differently, maybe I could have been Mrs. Fred Astaire.

Audrey Hepburn told me how she managed to stay so slim. She ordered everything she craved on the menu, but then would only take one bite. This satisfied her need to taste, but she didn't eat the whole thing. Who knew? One of these years I may try it.

When I was hired to do Funny Face, I was already in rehearsals for the musical Kiss Me Kate for the San Bernardino Civic Light Opera. Two great opportunities but, oh Lord, at the same time? Thank God I was young and survived the grueling schedule of daily 6 am studio calls and 7 pm rehearsals in San Bernardino. The only sleep I got was during lunch hour.

Opening night of Kate, curtain at eight! At 6 p.m. I was still on the soundstage at Paramount. I was in no position to tell Mr. Donen and Mr. Astaire, "I have to go now. I can't finish the scene." It was at least an hour drive to San Bernardino. I was panicking! I called the CLO producers, "I'll get there a.s.a.p.!" Would you believe they had the San Bernardino police meet me at the county line and escort us, sirens blaring to the stage door? On the ride over, I was in tears trying to put my makeup on, breathless and scared to death. That's show business! Most people suffer anxiety about going on stage. I was a nervous wreck about getting to the stage.

These were some of the curves and bumps beginning the show business adventure that is my life. I was asked once what it felt like to be a member of the Hollywood elite. I don't know that I've ever felt like a member of that club. I don't think that I've always "made the cut"... so to speak. I can say however that I've cut cards, lived, laughed and loved with those who are definitely club members. What a treat!

Chapter 5

My Screen Test Starred Frank Sinatra!

While diamonds are a girl's best friend, I have always preferred real estate! My first earnings went into land and my continuing earnings bought my first house in Palm Springs, the desert playground of the stars. I must correct myself. It was actually Darren "Mike Hammer" McGavin, who made the deal for which I happily paid. He and his wife were house shopping in the Racquet Club tract, where many other film and television people were buying get away homes. They found one for themselves and spotted one they thought was good for me. They were right. My neighbors turned out to be Steve McQueen, Mike Landon, Jackie Cooper, etc., etc. Those get away weekends were such fun. We'd hang out together, borrow sugar or booze from each other ... the laughs were so wonderful.

I had an especially good friend, Scotty Ruben. He was a genial host we called *Mr. Palm Springs*. Scotty surrounded himself with socially prominent, pretty and interesting people. I guess he thought I fell into one of those categories, because he would often invite me to join in. Scotty was a Chicago attorney, who had a great house in Palm Springs, where he entertained lavishly, as well as a penthouse on the Sunset Strip. He invited a group to the re-opening of *The Mocambo*, which had been the hot nightclub in Hollywood.

With the popularity of television, the club business had fallen on hard times. When owner, Charlie Morrison died, his wife Mary was trying to keep it going. She prevailed upon Frank Sinatra, who said, "I'll come in and play for a week. Vic Damone will play for a week. Dean Martin will play for a week and we'll see if we can get things going again."

It was Frank's opening night and luckily I was there. The place was jammed. Scotty had the front table. Frank was working on a small dais, in front of the stage, which was entirely filled with his orchestra.

I was too young to have appreciated Frank in his heyday at The Paramount in New York ... bobby soxers screaming and swooning. He was now doing the unrequited love songs and had another generation swooning. I watched Frank Sinatra totally mesmerized. Unless you've seen him live in performance, it might be hard to understand how captivating he was. But he was ... mesmerizing, sexy, intriguing and warm. That was Frank Sinatra's undeniable aura.

I sat there gazing up at him, my mouth hanging open. At some point during the evening, a waiter delivered a note to our host Scotty, from a gentleman and his wife asking to meet me.

Upon meeting, the gentleman said, "I'm Arthur Hornblow Jr. I am a producer. I have just given you a unique screen test. I watched you, watch Frank Sinatra and I think you would be a very good love interest for

Tyrone Power in my movie *Witness for the Prosecution*. Would you come in and meet the director, Billy Wilder?"

After I caught my breath, I said, "Is tomorrow too soon?" I went to the studio and met remarkable Billy Wilder. He put me on film ... shot me from a few angles and that was that.

I later heard, leading lady Marlene Dietrich, took one look at my film and said, "Nicht nein. Forget it! Like me, she's blonde." I was immediately called and became a brunette. I had the job. That's how I got *Witness for the Prosecution*. Thank you, Frank Sinatra. Thank you, Mr. Hornblow. And above all, thank you Jesus.

My first day on the film started after the company had been shooting for several weeks. Two stages at the Goldwyn studio had been turned into Old Bailey, the famous London courthouse, where all the big trials take place. The cast felt we were truly in Old Bailey. My first stop, before due on the set, was the makeup department. I was welcomed with open arms by guys I'd worked with many times before. I was also warned: "Honey, you'll be working with the great Charles Laughton. He's a nasty old faggot. He doesn't like young girls. You just do your work. Stay out of his way. Do what you have to do and everything will be fine."

CL – MD – TP – BW - Tea

I was a little nervous about the great Charles Laughton. I came onto the sound stage from the makeup department. Nobody said, "Hello or Welcome," or anything else. People around me went on with their business as usual. There was a group of famous actors sitting in a little British tea circle, sipping tea, not paying me any mind. For the first time in my life, I wished that the floor would open up and swallow me, because I didn't know what to do.

As I stood there in my skintight dress and perky little hat, by costume designer Grady Hunt, thinking, 'Oh dear, what do I do now? '... Someone smacked me hard on the rear end, sending me flying across the room. Looking back, I saw the great Charles Laughton, who loudly proclaimed, "That's the best damned ass I've seen in a long time!" Guess that tight little perky dress worked well ... as did all of the other costumes Grady did for me, for the rest of my career.

As for Charles Laughton, I became his little baby doll. He'd sulk if I didn't come in and say good morning to him, before I did anything else. He taught me to play Perquackey and Scrabble. We even did crossword puzzles. It was just an amazing relationship.

He and his wife, Elsa Lanchester, helped me greatly with that Middle English accent that was hard to achieve. It was marvelous to have theatre royalty help a newbie. Movie queen, Marlene Dietrich was mostly cool, make that "icy" and remote, with me. However, I envied her enduring star power and I truly admired her knowledge of camera and lighting. If she asked for a special highlight and the cinematographer didn't have it... she did! She carried a large trunk of special lighting. She knew what made her look good and insisted upon it.

Tyrone Power was warm and wonderful. Because I'd never seen his highly acclaimed movie, Blood and Sand, he arranged a screening for me. It was awesome to see him on the screen in full color while sitting next to me in full live color. He was a thoughtful generous star.

On *Witness*, they couldn't publicize me in the promotion of the movie, even though I would normally be the target for publicity, being the young hot chick. If they publicized me in the film, then it would be a giveaway of the surprise ending. Part of the big P.R. campaign was that the cast and crew signed nondisclosure agreements. We would not reveal the dramatic ending of the picture.

Tyrone Power and lucky me.

I was however promoted in another area. The makeup departments of our industry had for many years an event called the Deb Stars. Every year, each studio presented their young star of the future, United Artists presented me.

Deb Stars – me and my "competition"

The Deb Star event was a wonderful evening at the world-famous Palladium. Each young lady was escorted down the runway by a famous actor. I was thrilled to be on the arm of dashing Cesar Romero. He was by the way, a *very* good friend of Tyrone Power, our leading man. I'm happy to say that he was also a lifetime friend to me.

Some other Deb Stars were Joan Blackman, Barbara Lang, Joan Tabor, Rebecca Wells, Dolores Hart and Gloria Winters. Joan had a nice start at MGM. Barbara Lang was a beautiful lady, who died so young. Rebecca was a good actress, who was also famous for making beautiful, white lace dresses. Gloria was the ingénue on *Sky King*. Dolores gave up show business and became a nun. I marvel at that kind of transition. She is now the Prioress of Regina Laudis Abby in Connecticut. I'm confident that many of her prayers have been for those of us in show business.

None of these lovely girls continued an entertainment career that has lasted as long as mine. Perhaps, being blessed with versatility, I could do it all; acting, singing, dancing, talking, selling and saving ... my money. It was my role in *Witness* that led to being a Deb Star and other surprises. So once again, thank you Frank Sinatra for a wonderful evening and the serendipitous meeting with Arthur Hornblow Jr.

Chapter 6

Frank's Influence Continues

Frank Sinatra's idea of a good evening was a big Italian dinner at home with a bunch of friends and screening a new film. One evening that movie was *Witness for the Prosecution*.

At that time, he was in a production partnership with Howard Koch, who was a guest at Frank's that particular evening. I'd worked for Howard on many Warner Brothers projects; like *Maverick*, *Sugarfoot, 77 Sunset Strip* and *Cheyenne.* During the screening Frank said, "You know Howie, I've been watching this Ruta Lee chick on various things. She's kind of interesting. I think we should put her in one of our upcoming pictures." Howard agreed, "You couldn't have picked better, she's a favorite of mine."

Frank and I had never met at this point, nor was he aware that I had gotten the role in *Witness* thanks to him and his appearance at the Mocambo. Now I was the leading lady in his *Sergeants 3. T*alk about serendipity!!

Sergeants Three – The Rat Pack – 3 Crosby
boys on right – Buddy Lester above Ruta –
Hank Henry – Sonny King

Production began on *Sergeants 3* (a Western version of the classic Gunga Din). Frank sent his plane to bring me to the location in Kanab, Utah. While many Westerns had been shot there, this movie was the biggest thing to happen in a long time. I mean to have Frank Sinatra, Dean Martin, Sammy Davis Jr., Peter, Lawford, Joey Bishop, The Crosby Boys, Hank Henry and Henry Silva in one place. Wow! The bungalows at Parry's Lodge and every other hotel/inn were all taken by everyone associated with the movie. I got to the hotel and was shown to my room (which has since been named for me). I was then taken out to location.

This was the first time I met Frank. "Hello baby. How are you?" Again, I was mesmerized. His brilliant blue eyes and warm smile let me know I was welcome and part of the team right from the beginning.

Ruta and Webb. Ruta receiving her Utah's "Little Hollywood" plaque. In lieu of a star on the sidewalk, Kanab gave me a plaque on a real live hitchin' post.

During filming, each of the *Sergeants 3* stars (The Rat Pack) were also contracted to play one week at The Sands Hotel in Las Vegas. Director John Sturges had his hands full shooting around each missing star.

Kanab was a half hour flight to Vegas and Frank had a fleet of planes available. We went down for Frank's opening and a week later, the closing. We went down for Dean's opening and closing. We did this for the whole Rat Pack.

The shows were great fun. The boys always had a good time working. If Dean was performing, then Frank got up. Sammy then got up and everybody meandered in and out of the performances. It was just stupendous.

Around that time, Frank gave a birthday party for Dean. All of the Hollywood glitterati were there. We had about twenty people at our table; celebrities like John Wayne, Elizabeth Taylor, Milton Berle. It was an impressive group already, but this would be the first time that I ever saw or met Marilyn Monroe. She walked into that huge celebrity filled room on Frank's arm. My mouth just dropped. She glowed ... absolutely glowed. She had that same kind of radiance that the Gabor girls had ... that fabulous, wonderful aura, which makes someone shine. Marilyn had it. Even Elizabeth Taylor, being the beauty that she was, just disappeared in the glow of Marilyn. Maybe it was just being blonde, in a shimmering white dress and white fox. Regardless, all heads turned.

While we were shooting in Utah, Peter Lawford wanted to check his Palm Springs House. Frank said, "Take the plane." So, I also took the opportunity to check my little Palm Springs house. Well, somebody forgot to put ice on the plane. That's when I discovered how good vodka was straight! I was not a big drinker. I was more of mixed drinks person. I liked my MaiTai's, rum and coke and those girly drinks. So, Peter poured vodka and I sipped. Not bad. Somehow, Peter's stories got better the more I sipped. I wonder if his wife, Pat Kennedy, found him as engaging a raconteur as I did.

Back in Vegas, Frank didn't want me getting too chummy with Peter. I'm not too sure why. So, when he noticed this one-day at a party, he said, "It's late. You're going home." As a rule, it was Sammy's obligation to walk me to my room, whether in Kanab or Vegas. But this time, Frank escorted me to my room. He came in, sat and talked to me for a bit. We then hugged and kissed good night. The next thing I knew I was sort of being ushered toward the bedroom. All of the sudden, he pulled out his "masculinity." I took one look and gasped. It was huge. "I can't. I can't!" and started to cry. That was the end of even beginning to have an affair with him. From then on, he gave up on the sexy me and treated me like one of the family. Oh shit, maybe I could've been Mrs. Frank Sinatra!

On and off the set, the guys were always kidding around. We all had nicknames. Frank-Chairman, Sammy- Smokey and Dean - Drunky, who dubbed me Loudy. He claimed, "God didn't give Ruta breasts, he gave her a set of speakers."

Dean Martin-naturally funny/gracious
and wow can he sing.

Frank was the producer of the movie. On the set, he was known as "One-take-Sinatra." He'd say to the crew, "I don't care how long it takes you to set up the shot.

I'm going to give you a rehearsal and then set it up. Take all the time you need. Then I'm going to come in and I don't want to hear that there was a squeak on the dolly wheel. I don't want to hear that a light went out.

I don't want to hear that the sound didn't pick up. I want everything perfect. We're going to come in and do it for you once and that's it." That's a slight exaggeration. He might give you two takes. The rest of the time, it was fun and games."

They were always pulling pranks on each other, including throwing cherry bombs. So I said, "Hey guys, I've got an idea for Frank. When he goes out for lunch, I'm going to have his onstage dressing room filled with balloons, so when he opens the door he won't be able to get in. All of this was divinely funny until they started popping during takes ... very costly disruption. Ouch! my mistake. Those guys were really good to me. Before leaving the studio after work for dinner with an agent friend, Marvin Moss, I went to the ladies' room to fluff up a little bit. Inadvertently, I left my ring on the washbasin.

While at dinner, I remembered, 'Oh my goodness I left my pretty ring. 'I went back and it was gone. Frank heard about it. A couple of days later on the set, Frank said, "Hey Loudy come here."

Peter – Sammy – Dean – Frank… trust me,
that's not milk!

I saw all the guys giggling and whispering. 'Hmmm,' I
thought, 'Oh, they're going to do something terrible to
me. They're going to put a firecracker up my dress.'
The next thing I knew, there's the Rat Pack and they
say, "TADA!" and hand me a box from Van Cleef. There
was the most glorious south sea pearl ring, huge… the
size of a nickel. It was surrounded by diamonds. I burst
into tears… they burst into smiles, a great unforgetable
moment.

The interiors were shot in Hollywood at Goldwyn Studios. Sometimes Frank would say, "Hey Loudy, come on to the house. I'll buy you dinner." He respected and trusted me enough to share some of his most private and painful feelings.

It was during these quiet evenings that I got to know the melancholy Frank that was normally covered by Chairman of the board bravura.

His stories about Ava Gardner and unrequited love still break my heart. His never-ending love for his family was a joy to listen to. I was glad for him, but sad for me and all the girls when he became engaged to Juliet Prowse. That lasted a scant few months.

Frank had a wonderful, big compound in Palm Springs, but one night he came over to my itty-bitty Palm Springs house for dinner. Songwriter, composer Arthur Hamilton (Cry Me a River, Is That All There Is?) and his wife, Mitzi, were staying with me. Frank called and said, "Hey Loudy. Do you want to do dinner?" I said, "Frank, why don't you come over here for a change?" He said, "O.K."

Well, that sent the three of us into a panic. How do we prepare? I didn't have all of those nice things that he did in his home. My plates were Melmac. We went out and bought steak and all in all created a great dinner. Having Frank in my tiny abode was comfortable, entertaining and unforgettable.

Ever-generous Frank brought over six bottles of Chateauneuf-du-Pape. We drank some and we put away the rest of the treasure to save for some monumental occasion. Those unopened bottles remained where we left them for years. Mind you, they were in a closet where temperatures could reach 115 degrees.

Some twelve years later, my engagement to Webb was the occasion I'd been saving them for. I was hoping they wouldn't be vinegar. To my surprise nothing had changed. It just got better. It was like drinking velvet. Once again, "Thank you Frank."

I was a regular at Frank's Palm Springs home. One time I went over and Bing Crosby was there. Bing remembered me. It was thrilling once again to be with the masters of the song and just me sitting there like a little twerp listening to both of them carry on.

Frank knew that I was politically, very conservative. All of his life, he had been a staunch democrat who created and performed huge events for the party, especially Jack Kennedy. However, he was really hurt by Mr. Kennedy. Frank had gone to a great deal of effort, equipping the Sinatra Compound with Secret Service, security and communication necessities for a Presidential visit. The President chose to stay at Bing Crosby's estate. I don't know for what reasons, but I know how deeply hurt Frank was.

His love of God, family and country brought Frank to a more conservative political ideology. He became a big

Ronald Reagan fan and friend. I too, have always leaned toward conservatism. Well, hell I'm right of Attila the Hun.

I was on the campaign trail with the Nixons, the Reagans and the Murphys. Amazingly enough, I debated in public venues, some very interesting Hollywood people. Among them were Warren Beatty and Dennis Weaver.

At that time, one of Frank's best buddies was Nixon's Vice President, Spiro Agnew. I was often invited to join the Agnews at Frank's. The conversations and discussions were engaging and most certainly, enlightening. This was the time Frank was beginning to see Barbara Marx, who later became the last Mrs. Sinatra.

I was president of *The Thalians* and prevailed upon Sammy Davis to be our honoree at the annual Thalians All-Star Ball. I also prevailed upon Frank, our former honoree to present Sammy, the Disney designed, "Mr. Wonderful" Award. He said, "Sure baby. I'll be there." "Great! Thank you ... who are you going to bring?" He answered, "Well, dummy, I'm bringing you."

So now he's my date, he's going to present; he's going to sing – I hit the trifecta!! Two days before the event my father, on a hunting trip, was suddenly killed in an automobile accident in Canada. I was frantic about putting a ball and funeral together. We literally put my father on ice until the Gala was over. Thalians Chairman Debbie Reynolds, was on Broadway in

Irene and wasn't able to take over. I was running the whole thing. I then got a call from Frank's secretary. With no explanation or anything, she said, "Frank won't be there."

I thought Good God. How much more can I take? I'm talking to the Canadian Mounties about getting my father's body here. Horrible stuff is going on. Nobody is answering me about why Frank isn't coming. What am I supposed to say to the press? I never got an answer. What could I do?

I have to explain to you first, that Hollywood Columnist Rona Barrett (one of my dearest friends) had become persona non grata with Frank. You know, he ran hot and cold with people, very flammable. For years, she had been like a kid in his family... best friend to his daughter Nancy. Something happened. Rona reported or printed something that Frank took the wrong way and she was ostracized. However, she and I continued to be absolutely good friends. He was probably aware of that. Rona and I went to a Nixon White House event in San Clemente. Frank threatened to push her in the pool. I got her out of there before he could.

Back to *The Thalians* event, where Sammy commented that Frank was originally to sing, "My Way." But he did it instead, hit a high note and said, "Eat your heart out Frank." The audience loved being in on the joke. Naturally, Rona and all the press commented on Frank's absence.

I got a letter from Frank saying, "Next time you need somebody to help you with your charity, go to your good friends from the press like Rona Barrett and Army (Variety) Archerd. I didn't even know what he was talking about. What was he blaming me for? I sent a letter back saying, "What are you talking about? What have I done to deserve your wrath?"

He did not speak to me for a long time. I never got answers back when I reached out to him, never got a word. I talked to his secretary, she'd fill me in ... tiny little bits, because she was aware of how quickly he could get pissed.

Well, it turned out the reason he did not come or offer any explanation was the shit was hitting the fan for his very good friend, Spiro Agnew. It was all extremely hush, hush. Frank had flown to Baltimore to be with the Agnews, as charges were being leveled at the Vice President. Frank was there to add support. None of us knew this, because he chose not to say anything while it was going on.

One night, a year later, I walked into *Pips* (a backgammon club). Frank was sitting at the bar and I gasped. I didn't know what to do. As I walked in, he looked at me. It was too late to retreat. I'd been spotted. Much to my relief, Frank opened his arms and said, "Hey Loudy. How's my baby?" There was never any discussion about what happened. We just let it be. I didn't see him as much, because he was married at this point, but we always stayed friendly. I also remained friendly with

Frank's family. Nancy Sr. will always remain an outstanding beautiful and generous lady. My pal, Little Nancy chaired *The Thalians* Ball when I was the honoree. Her sister, Tina helped produce the show and Frank Jr. performed. Clearly Frank's generosity gene was passed on to his children.

All these years later, I'm still in touch with the Sinatra family. I will forever be profoundly grateful for the role that Frank and family played in my life and career.

I need to mention when Rona retired to her ranch in Santa Ynez, she took on the most important work of her life. Using her celebrity and work ethic she founded and built Golden Inn and Village, a phenomenal residence for lower income seniors of every size, shape and color. I am very proud of my "lil sis."

Chapter 7

I Love Lucy!

Ruta – Lucille Ball – Sammy Davis Jr. 2 legends on
our stage and in our lives

There was television before *Lucy and* television after
Lucy. "After" was never the same. She forever changed
the cultural landscape. Now an audience found a woman
both beautiful and funny. With her strong business savvy,
she proved that women could lead in any industry.

I did maybe five or six of Lucy's productions that included
The Lucy Show, Here's Lucy and several specials. People

often asked me how it was to work with Lucy. I believe it's complimentary to say that she was a very, very demanding taskmaster. She would brook no foolishness. I mean she'd laugh at things, but as a rule when she worked, she worked. With Lucy, you couldn't take it personally. If she barked, "You're not standing on your mark; move over." That's all it meant. You didn't have to worry about, 'Oh damn -- am I doing the wrong thing? Is she going to fire me?'

I learned a lot by watching her work the four-camera system. You really have to be so precise on your marks when you're dealing with four moving cameras, because your nose could be in the shot, when the camera is on somebody else, or vice versa. The rehearsals had to be precise, like choreographing a dance. Lucy liked working with me because I could do exactly what she wanted every time.

She was older than I, but liked having some younger broads around, who were fun. Lucy loved to laugh and surrounded herself with people that kept her laughing. Barbara Stuart, Carol Burnett, protégé Carole Cook and me, (funny ladies) were among the regulars invited to her house to play charades. She loved all games, but became obsessed with backgammon, so our charade get-togethers became less frequent.

But whatever the game, God forbid you went to Lucy's house hungry. You'd think being married to a Jewish man—Gary Morton, at that time—that the refrigerator would have been stocked with salami, cheese, ham, rye bread, bagels and cream cheese. Nope. You'd see maybe three pieces of celery and a piece of bologna. That was a big treat. She just wasn't into food.

Maybe in her family growing up, food wasn't the center of things. I grew up in a family where it was: *First we'll eat. Later we'll talk.* There was always food and drink for company. Clearly Lucy wasn't aware of that rule ... an amusing surprise to me.

I first met Lucy years earlier when I was taken to Del Mar racetrack in California by a mutual friend. Can you imagine my excitement when I was invited to join Lucy and Desi in their box? I was in awe of Lucy. She was struck by my polka dot dress (which was part of the "Lucy look"). In fact, she always liked what I wore. One rainy day I was wearing a see-through plastic raincoat. It was piped in white and very pretty. She loved it -- so I immediately ran out and got her one. She also loved my extensive collection of costume jewelry, which she would borrow on occasion. Sometimes I'd have to say, "Hey girlfriend. Can I borrow it back?" To this day, when I wear some of those pieces, I proudly think, 'This was around my Lucy's neck.' So were her beautiful silk scarves that little Lucie gave me when her mom died.

Little Lucie attended Immaculate Heart High school, my former alma mater. Big Lucy asked Barbara Stuart (Gomer Pyle's Miss Bunny) and me to see Little Lu in her school production of *Annie Get Your Gun.* We thought she was wonderful. Clearly talent is in the genes.

Little Lucie became our friend as well. At her short-lived wedding to Phil Vandervoort, we were all in attendance at the Beverly Hill's family home. Her mom was now married to Gary Morton – a well-known comic and clotheshorse. Desi Arnaz, father of the bride, was to escort his daughter down the aisle. She had been dressing in the master bedroom, which Desi certainly knew well. When he observed Gary's newly expanded and meticulously arranged dressing area, he exclaimed with his familiar Cuban accent, "Whatz the fuck is dis Sy-Devore West?" (Devore was clothier to the stars)

I more recently saw little Lu at the Hollywood Museum, for Lucy's 100th birthday celebration. She looked absolutely beautiful and has been happily married to fine actor, Laurence Luckinbill for over forty years. We joyfully reminisced about *The Thalians* 30th Anniversary - *THE LUCILLE BALL* – honoring her mother. We *Thalians* are famous for our extravagant all-star shows. *The Lucille Ball* was no exception. From an opening act with elephants and carousel of ponies, to a marching band and balloon drop finale, it was colossal. The most fun for us was the comedy sketch - which featured Little Lu as Lucy, Little Desi as Ricky, Shecky Greene as Fred Mertz and me as Ethel. This was just one of the times I asked Lucy to make a charitable appearance. She never turned me down.

It was really lovely and a sweet feather in my cap to be invited as *guest star* for the annual Lucy's Birthday Memorial held in her birthplace, Jamestown, New York. Thousands of people come in from all over the world for this event. The crowds go to see where she was born and where she is buried (next to her mom). They also come to meet the people who were involved in her life. They had wonderful clips of the Lucy shows that I guest starred on and talked about during *An Evening with Ruta Lee*. It was inspiring to realize that my dear friend Lucy remained so important in the lives of millions - who never met her or *loaned her jewelry*.

Lucy was beautiful before and after she became a comedy icon. She started out as a showgirl, turned dramatic actress, turned comedienne. The rest is history—and I feel so blessed to have witnessed it from the front row.

Ruta as Ethel – Desi Jr. as Ricky – Lucie as Lucy and Shecky as Fred

Chapter 8

"What's Thalians?"

Star Studded, That's What!

I often wonder if the publicity around my philanthropy caused Hollywood directors and producers to regard me as a dilettante, rather than a serious actress. Maybe they thought my interests were only charitable and social. Perhaps it got in the way of being hired more often.

To me, giving is receiving. I've been giving my time and energy to *The Thalians* for over half a century. This organization began with a group of young stars that were tired of being considered pot smoking, hard drinking, sex minded, young idiots, with nothing to contribute. They said, "We get together, we party, we dance, we sing around the piano. Why don't we invite the public, sell a few tickets and raise a few dollars for charity?" That's how *The Thalians* was born. Named after Thalia, a muse and Greek goddess of comedy.

Some of the founding members were Jayne Mansfield (mother of Mariska Hargitay), George Schlatter (*Laugh-In*) and Hugh O'Brian (Wyatt Earp). Jayne and Mamie Van Doren were sent out to find a worthy cause to support. They came back and in inimitable blonde bombshell manner, said, "All the good diseases are taken." However, they found Dr. Judd Marmor, who was dealing with emotionally disturbed children. He said, "An emotionally disturbed child is like a rotten apple in a barrel. The whole community can be affected." And he was doing something about it. So, *The Thalians* took on the cause of children's mental health. Eighteen years later we built and opened *The Thalians* Community Mental Health Center, the first building to go in at The Cedars Sinai, Complex where we expanded to encompass care from pediatric to geriatric.

I became involved with *The Thalians* early in my career. I became enamored with this organization when, at one of their first fund- raisers, I saw their parody of *The King and I* with Donald O'Connor as the king, the Crosby boys as the princes and 5 by 5 Comedienne Muriel Landers as Anna—Oh what laughs! This was a group I had to be part of! I went to some of their meetings, eventually got nominated and elected to the board. However, I was traveling a great deal, because I was working on stage, in television or a movie somewhere, thereby missing many meetings ... so they took me off the board, kicked me upstairs and made me a vice president—looked good and I didn't have that many meetings to attend.

Debbie Reynolds, who was president, kept her eye on me. She noticed when I was assigned a responsibility, I fulfilled it and that was that. I learned a great deal from her. Here she was a big star, a constantly working actress, wife to shoe magnate Harry Karl, mother to Carrie and Todd and still, she made time for *The Thalians*. She was also the most generous person I'd ever met.

We'd meet quite often and sit on her big, king-sized bed, with her notes and papers spread all around (which she did to her final day). I'd sit and talk to her about things necessary to our fundraising efforts, the need for auction items, raffle prizes, etc. She'd say, "Go over to such and such jeweler. Say Harry Karl buys a lot of stuff here and you've got to give us something. I'd do as she said and report to her. I learned from Debbie you can ask anybody for anything if it isn't for yourself – but for charity.

Some of our Thalians boosters – Janet Leigh – Ann Miller – James Stewart – Debbie – Charlton Heston – Ruta and Jerry Franks - producer

The Thalians went on to become exceptionally successful. Each year, the board selected an honoree, who not only dazzled us with their performances on stage and screen, but with their philanthropy as well. We built each year's event, around that honoree, with every available star doing hilarious sketches and take offs on the honoree's movies.

After *The King and I*, we did a parody on La Dolce Vita, starring our own buxom Jayne Mansfield. Next, we did a take-off on the James Bond films. Every star in town was willing to play a little part. It was amazing what went on. You can imagine how thrilled I was to have members like Edward G. Robinson, Agnes Moorehead, Jack Lemmon and Ricardo Montalban doing sketches – and dancers like Juliet Prowse, Rita Moreno, Shirley Jones, Sally Struthers and Lucille Ball to fill the Chorus line – and producers like George Schlatter and Jack Haley Jr. to put the whole thing together.

Hotelier, Conrad Hilton, was one of our mentors. We held our early events at the *Beverly Hilton* for many years. He would give us rooms for our general membership meetings and provide hors d'oeuvres and such – which brought a lot of young people into the hotel. It was good for The Hilton and it was good for us. Everybody in Hollywood wanted to be part of *The Thalians*.

Most board meetings were held at Debbie's home that she shared with Harry Karl. Her Chinese house couple would prepare some exotic meal for us—very fancy. Her beautiful house on the LA Country Club Golf Course eventually was lost, when she inherited the multi-million-dollar debt, her gambler husband left her. Never giving bankruptcy a serious thought, Debbie sang and tapped danced her way out of that debt ... It took years. Bravo Debbie!

Anyway, like any family, in spite of disagreements and bickering, we were a tight knit group – a family with highs and lows. At one of our meetings, we experienced a tragic low together, when our CFO and also my accountant, Bill Gold, had a fatal heart attack. Debbie's Girl Scout training kicked right in and she started doing CPR, while I rubbed his wrists, waiting for the paramedics. Bill is still missed 'til this day. His memory was later honored with a star on our celebrity walk of fame at *The Thalians Mental Health Center.* This was generously donated by his brother, David Gold, founder of the *99 Cent* stores. Appropriately, he gave us a check for $999,999.99 cents.

Hugh O'Brien was our first Thalians' president, followed by singer Margaret Whiting and then Debbie, who stayed on for several years, before pulling in her *Singing in the Rain,* costar Donald O'Connor as president. He was a darling man, but he was "on the road" too much to be effective in a leadership position.

We needed to find a replacement. A meeting was called, and several big-name stars were suggested. Then Debbie said, "I have the perfect person ... Ruta Lee!" Well, I almost fainted. I never expected anything like this. Debbie held sway ... they voted, and I was in.

To this day, it's the most challenging role that I've ever played. Running an organization is infinitely more difficult than learning a script. I was president for at least fourteen years. Debbie then said, "I plan to be home for a while, so let's move you up to Chairman of the Board and I'll be President." So, we switched roles. Ha! Let's put it this way, plans change, and Debbie was back on the road again, paying off her next husband's debts.

She was my sister in charity, my mentor, best friend and continues to be an inspiration. She believed in paying back and forward, all blessings. That's also part of my life credo. When I think of how tough life was for her, that she and her kids were literally living in her car, because she was so damn broke and that she survived it all with grace, dignity and humor ... Wow! What's sad is that I didn't know what was going on. She never complained. It breaks my heart that I didn't realize—when I could've helped her... when I could've said, "Move in with us!"

When Debbie was on Broadway, starring in *Irene*, in which she was brilliant, I went to see her. We went out after the show and had Mexican food (her favorite). We talked honestly about a lot of things. She was so appreciative of how I was handling *The Thalians*, a big load off her back. She was the first to say, "Without Ruta, *The Thalians* would have crumbled long ago." So there I was, acting as both President and Chairman of the Board for the next thirty years. All those wonderful years of hard work were worth the sweat, when it turned into the sweet smell of $ucce$$ for the Mental Health Clinic. I have endless gratitude to the luminaries that I called on year after year – to fill our stage with entertainment, our hearts with joy and our seats with generous donors. Our more than fifty years of honorees is the "who's who" of American entertainment, all gifted, gracious and generous with their precious time.

The selection process for honorees went like this. The board, after much discussion, would narrow down to two or three names that were deserving of the Mr./Ms. Wonderful award (a statue of Goofy, created for *The Thalians*, by Walt Disney). We selected stars who dazzled us, not only with their screen and stage performances, but with their philanthropic performances as well. Now, it was up to Debbie or me to make the approaches. Of course, stars never know their schedules too far in advance.

So, quite often, I'd reach out to one star and Debbie another. Then, we'd play the waiting game and hope that one of us would come back with a positive answer--so we could get the "ball rolling." There were indeed times we thought we might have double honorees and there were also times that we didn't have an honoree until practically ball time ... WHEW!!

It was my friendship with Lucy that got her as an honoree. I also landed "Mr. Entertainment", Sammy Davis Jr. I asked Angela Lansbury, while I was doing an episode of *Murder She Wrote*. As usual, it took some persuasion, but she accepted.

Rip Taylor – Lesley Uggams – Ron Masak – Debbie
Reynolds – Jerry Herman – John Schneider – Angela
Lansbury – Bea Arthur - Ruta

That year the only ballroom available was on October
31st. We all panicked. I said, "Wait a minute." Why don't
we take advantage of Halloween and make it a Venetian
masked ball? We asked everybody to come in black tie
and to wear a beautiful mask. It worked. It was just
gorgeous. When I stop and think of the people that I
booked to perform for all of our honorees—I'm awed at
my own salesmanship! It was really extraordinary.

Early in the game, before I knew him, Debbie got Frank Sinatra. Not only did he consent to be the honoree but volunteered to perform and even picked up the cost for the entire orchestra. No wonder, he was known as Mr. Generous.

Debbie also got Gene Kelly, with whom I had the pleasure of sharing a bed ... in the movie *Marjorie Morningstar*. He sometimes rented my Palm Springs house, so you might say we occupied the same bed twice.

When I got Gene's good friend and colleague, Fred Astaire to be a guest at my table, Jack Haley Jr., our director, recognizing a golden opportunity, asked me to prevail upon Fred to present the Mr. Wonderful Award to Gene Kelly, culminating the show. I did indeed ask Fred and he shyly declined.

The production table was on the opposite side of the huge ballroom, so I hoisted my layers of chiffon and ran through the work spattered Century Plaza kitchen, careful not to slip--and relayed the disappointing response to our producers. I then ran the same route back to my table to find that Fred had now reconsidered and perhaps would agree. Again, I ran back to the production table to give them the good news—and then back to my own table again, only to find that Fred was once again vacillating. At that point, I think he took pity on an exhausted me and did indeed present the award to Gene. It was worth the five-hundred-yard dash. What a perfect finale ... two legendary dance stars on our stage, thanks to my not slipping on my ass in the kitchen. Gene's lovely widow

Patricia Ward Kelly is keeping Gene's presence alive with her one-woman show about the iconic legend.

There are so many stories about the hundreds of big star entertainers involved with *The Thalians*, but it all boils down to the fact that they liked our charity Hollywood for Mental Health and gave their time to the two ladies responsible for it.

Back Row L-R Jimmy Baker – Producer Janet Leigh - Gene Kelly – Ruta - Jack Haley Jr. - Producer Front Row – Ann Miller – Debbie – Betty Garrett – Gloria De Haven

As *The Thalians* became known on a global scale, the Italian Ministry of Culture invited us to produce the prestigious Rome based, *Rudolph Valentino Awards in Hollywood*. The solid gold statuette of Valentino was presented to internationally renowned film stars. The recipients were always gracious, grateful and humble ... with a few exceptions. Let's dish!

I've always greatly admired Lauren Bacall on stage and screen. However, along with her baggage, came a lot of attitude ... at this event anyway. For starters, she wouldn't fly out from New York on first class tickets that had been donated to us by *American Airlines,* insisting instead on the uber expensive *MGM Grand* (a now defunct airline). She would not stay in the Presidential Suite (gratis) at the *Century Plaza*-where the event was taking place. *N*o, she had to stay at the Bel Air Hotel and her hairdresser, who flew with her also at our expense, had to stay at the Beverly Hills Hotel. This meant that we had to provide limousine transportation for both, to and from the hotels. Ching, Ching, Ching ... many dollars adding up!! Well, the night of the event, she arrived, looking like a hairdresser had never touched her hair. She was also in a gown that hadn't been pressed. The saving grace was that she was well received by our patrons.

Lauren was so nervous, as she got up to go on stage that she was trembling like a leaf. I couldn't help but smirk. I knew she was shaking, because she grabbed my hand. Later, I read her book and I gleaned from it, that she had many difficulties and not all her life was easy. Who knows? Maybe she was super insecure about being an honoree, which could explain the behavior. If so, I apologize.

Speaking of attitude, handsome, Valentino honoree, Sylvester Stallone threw some our way. After a sumptuous Italian dinner, he was anxious to get the show moving. Our show had been delayed a little, because a border curtain near one of the lights started to smoke. It was however quickly extinguished. During the fracas, Sylvester sent one of his minions backstage to inform us that he had lost patience and was leaving. I don't know where I got the chutzpah, but I said, "Fine! Let him leave!! He will suffer the embarrassment in the press, not us." ... He stayed.

Margie Petersen/Charlton Heston/Ruta
and Debbie

When the show curtains opened, the enchanting Howard Keel, our star performer walked out on the white fire-retardant spattered stage. He exclaimed, "Who's throwing all this shit? I haven't even sung yet?" Thankfully, Sylvester's humor kicked in and he was a humbled and grateful honoree.

Bette Davis gave attitude better than anybody, but coming from her, it was fabulous. Ms. Davis was in her golden years when she was our Valentino honoree. This diminutive dynamo was a little shaky and nervous when it was time to receive her award. She clung to me and said in her all too familiar intonation, "Rutaahh, Staaay with me. Don't let me make a fool of myself." Bette was no fool. She was one of the most eloquent and fascinating speakers that we ever had on our stage. She said how thrilled and how appropriate it was to be receiving the Valentino statuette. She recalled, that as young girls, she and her sisters were permitted to go to the cinema on Saturday afternoons. She would be thrilled beyond description, seeing "The Sheik", Rudolph Valentino, gallop across the moonlit desert sands on a white stallion, dismount, fling open the drapes of the tent, approach the heavy breathing damsel, reach down, undressing her by removing her slipper, pour wine into it and drink. Ahhhhhh ... What romance! At which point in our evening, Charlton Heston, the ultimate gentleman, sitting directly below Bette, reached up, took the Maud Frizon slipper off her foot, filled it with Champaign and drank. The audience exploded! A true Hollywood moment--and damn it--not one photographer got the picture. Obviously, this was long before cell phones.

Rejection is something that every performer must learn to accept and live with. However, in charity, one must never take "no" for an answer. For some twenty years, I hounded Clint Eastwood to be our *Thalians* honoree.

He'd always say, "No Roots, I can't do it. I'm going to be on a film. I'm going to be in another country." Finally I said, "Listen, next week, May 30th is my birthday. I want a present. Make my day! Say yes!! And I will never bother you again." He replied, "The 31st is my birthday! You make my day and let me off the hook." I didn't. Finally, he gave in ... and what a wonderful honoree he was!

Like Clint, most celebrities are reticent in agreeing to our request. Many feel there will be a responsibility to solicit their friends and business associates to participate in making the event a financial success. We made it easy for our honorees and told them, "You don't have to do a damn thing. Just show up looking handsome/beautiful, greet the press, wave to your friends and adoring fans, then sit down and enjoy an evening of music, love and laughter, dedicated to you, by your peers."

Even tougher than getting the honoree, was putting the event together at minimal cost, so that proceeds went directly to our clinic. Each event took a full year to produce. *The Thalians* always took great pride in getting everything "free." Show people are the most generous with their time and talent. They donate to charity the only thing they have to sell. However, the live and silent auctions, public relations, décor, transportation, food, rehearsals, music, running a three-ring circus was costly. Every year I had to go out and find somebody to cough up a hundred thousand dollars to underwrite the ball. I worked very hard and learned a lot. Hell, I could have run *General Motors*—without the damn bail out.

Each year we tried to top the previous year. In 2001, when I was chosen as honoree by the board and ball chair, Nancy Sinatra, I too understood the reticence of previous honorees. I truly did not feel that I deserved any such honor. I also didn't think that I was a big enough star to sell out the ball. I was no Lana Turner or Whoopi Goldberg, but with Nancy and Tina Sinatra's urging, reluctantly I agreed.

Several weeks before our scheduled ball, tragedy befell our country... the 9/11 bombings. The nation was in mourning. We considered cancelling our event. Nancy, our underwriters, Paula Kent Meehan (Redken) and Wallace Annenberg insisted we go forward, as we would need some light and laughter at this bleak time. They were right! In spite of my fears and trepidations, I received so much more than the Ms. Wonderful Award and applause. I recognized the overwhelming gift of respect, love and appreciation from my community, as this 45th Annual Ball, turned out to be our most successful event and the biggest moneymaker in our history. Thank you to all who participated in my honor and all *Thalians* events. You filled my heart and life with joy and gratitude.

All of our events had the most amazing shows. One that stands out was for Robert Preston. We had Mary Martin performing *Flaming Agnes, from I Do, I Do,* Barry Bostwick and Barbara Eden doing *Mack and Mable*, darling Shirley Jones doing *Music Man* and the inimitable Lucy doing *Mame*—with a line of handsome chorus boys, including my Godson, Scott Deshong! What a line up!

Debbie – Carol Channing – Carol Lawrence – Mary
Martin – Jane Wyman – Ruta – Florence
Henderson... What a blessing... all my girlfriends

We did a beautiful show when Mary Martin was our honoree. Ray Walston and I did Honey Bun from *South Pacific*. You can guess how nervous I was doing Mary's number for Mary. All participants in our shows, be they wardrobe people, hairdressers, performers, stage managers, etc. gave their time and talent gratis, for the love of the charity and the honoree.

When I think about the "now generation", all I can say is, "Thank you Dr. Spock" (and not darling Leonard Nimoy). You created a "What's in it for me generation?" that does not believe in paying it back or forward. I'm generalizing of course. There are some profoundly wonderful, generous young people that are out there and willing to give their time and money to a worthy cause.

As for the others, maybe they just haven't found a bandwagon to jump on. When *The Thalians* has reached out to young people, their reps say, "Send a private plane. They'll be a party of twelve at the event. You'll have to house and feed everyone. We'll have to bring the conductor and all of the musicians. You will be sending limousines ... and of course there will be a Rolex watch!" ... which leaves no money for the charity. Now, if you can get to the celebrity on a face-to-face basis, there most likely would not be a problem. However, with most young celebrities, there's a phalanx of protection, starting with agent, business manager, lawyer, hairdresser, masseuse and trainer.

The managers and agents aren't the least bit interested in helping, as there is no salary to get their percentage from. Publicists may be interested because they think it could be a good P.R. opportunity. However, these days, most publicists are hired to keep the press away from the star.

Today, young people do not grow up hearing and believing that you have to give something back. They don't ascribe to "share your blessings." A few young people have stepped forward such as Billy Morrison, Camp Freddy, Taylor Dane, Clint Black and his wife Lisa Hartman. I cornered her in the bathroom once to ask her to join us. She and Clint came through.

I've certainly had my share of recognition for my Thalians work. Gloria Luchenbill started our Thalians magazine, which was distributed internationally and is in the Library of Congress. She had been an editor for several movie magazine's in New York and LA—and boy, did she know P.R. She knew how to add glamour and pizazz to our organization and make us really important. Because of her, I became a philanthropic entity in the community, rather than just being a movie person, semi-star. *The Thalians* and Ruta Lee became synonymous.

If I failed *The Thalians* in any way, it's that I couldn't find young show business personalities to replace Debbie and myself. The celebs that I did ask said, "No." They didn't want the responsibility and I didn't have the time to make recruitment my goal. I did try. I wanted Sally Field to take over, but she was involved in too many other things. So, I prevailed upon a Board Member, my dear friend Dr. Erwin Lehrhoff, to take over running the organization. He is an eminent psychologist, businessman and founder of *The Thalians* President's Club. In his and our Board of Directors' capable hands, we continue to accomplish miracles.

After fifty-five years, *The Thalians* moved from the Cedars-Sinai campus. Our building, renamed The Thalians Health Center, remains as a solid tribute to our early members and supporters, who built and maintained it, as a center for Mental Health. Sadly, today it is no longer a *Mental* Health Center. Cedars- Sinai administrators, in their bias judgement, found other more profitable uses for it. Unfortunately, our Thalians endowment of multimillions also remains with Cedars-Sinai, in perpetuity. We fervently hope that someday it will once again provide continued treatment and research in mental health for which all the millions of dollars of contributions were intended.

Since its inception, *The Thalians* has been a spotlight shining on the darkness of mental disease, bringing it into the light of healing. We have recently changed the focus of that spotlight and are now shining it on a profound need ... that of our returning veterans. We owe them a great debt of gratitude and they deserve the best care that America can provide. Therefore, we are now devoting our efforts to Operation Mend at UCLA, our new home. Operation Mend founder Ron Katz, Dr. Timothy A. Miller (People's Man of the Year), Dr. Kodi K. Azari, Director Dr. Tom Strouse, Dr. Jo Sornborger and their amazing teams, are the angels healing our wounded warriors broken bodies. We Thalians are concerned with healing the broken mind and spirit. Our first fundraiser for Operation Mend was held at the infamous Playboy Mansion. It was the hottest ticket in town. Some of Hugh Hefner's bunnies were pretty hot too. I must tell you folks that Hugh was more than a Playboy businessman, as he has given millions to various charitable causes.

It was inspiring to share that evening at the mansion, with many of our wounded warriors. One of them was the charming Marine Corporal, Aaron P. Mankin, the first *Operation Mend* patient (his face, hands body, severely burned in a bomb blast).

Aaron, who has endured countless reconstructive surgeries, took the mic and quipped, "It's nice to look out over a Hollywood crowd and see more plastic surgery than I've had."

At our next fab event held at the House of Blues in Hollywood, we honored the legendary Smokey Robinson, in a musical star-studded evening. The Emmy wining Kira Lorsch and her late husband Bob produced the fantastic event. It was a far cry from our black-tie ball room evenings and introduced *The Thalians* to a younger hip crowd. Some of the wonderful people that assist *The Thalians* in person and purse are on our Board of Governors.

Ruta/Margie and our remarkable Dr. Piro

My dearest dynamic girlfriend Jackie Rosenberg is not only a great asset to my personal life and welfare but to *The Thalians* and Op Mend every day in every way.

For over 60 years my beautiful, inside and out, gal pal, Sandy Krause has supported my efforts with love and *big bucks* through all those years. Bill and Pat Anton, my forever friends, self-made magnates dazzled the food service industry with their innovative airport enterprises.

They are with us and support us all the way. Dr. Lawrence Piro keeps my life on track in every way and supports all our efforts. My blonde beauty Madeline Gussman, when needed, had the smarts, pizazz and brains to take over the Aerospace and Defense business she and husband Marvin had built. She continues their generous contributions to many charitable organizations. I thank God and Madeline for her ongoing support to *The Thalians* and Op Mend.

So, with the help of Governors/Board/Patrons , the beat goes on. While I have stepped down to chairman emeritus, I'll always be there to help and assist...so will our beloved Debbie in spirit.

We are Thalians forever!

Chapter 9

I'm in the Service Now! "USO"

Roger Miller – Ruta – Sheb Wolley...good times
with super performers

Anyone who knows me also knows that I have a deep and abiding love the USA. It has provided me and my family with countless blessings, for which I will be forever grateful! Needless to say, I was excited and delighted when asked to tour with the USO and later work for Armed Forces Radio and Television Services (AFRTS). I was honored that I got to add a little touch of fun and laughter to the lives of our service personnel worldwide, who risk everything for us.

The two years I spent with the AFRTS were extraordinary. I hosted radio shows that aired all over Europe and Asia. The servicemen loved it. So did I! I also did television commercials on how to package and mail things to our military. I became a sort of pinup girl for these guys. They would see me on television in my miniskirt and boots, then they'd hear me chatting and playing their favorite kinds of music, jazz, early rock and country. It was a great music lesson for me, because until then, I was not familiar with these recording artists. However, I learned in a unique way through the joy of interviewing and recording some of the biggest names in music ... the likes of 'Mountain High', John Denver, 'King of The Road', Roger Miller, 'Wichita Lineman', Glen Campbell and the legendary Lou Rawls ... who fancied me. (Just think, I could have been Mrs. Lou Rawls.) I came into the AFRTS studios once or twice a week, recorded five or six shows, that would be transmitted overseas and played daily. Bill Ezzell conceived and produced these shows. His love of country music was the inspiration and foundation for the now very prestigious, Country Music Awards.

I've mentioned Johnny Grant, presiding over my star ceremony earlier. Johnny (honorary Mayor of Hollywood) alternated USO shows with Bob Hope, where we toured in the Philippines, Pacific Islands, Hawaii and Greenland. Many were Christmas tours. I enjoyed meeting the young men, spending time with them, hanging out in the mess halls and having Christmas dinners together.

One Christmas, our troupe spent the day on a black sand beach at Subic Bay, Philippines. My dance partner and I decided to take a walk off the hot sands and into the cool, lush tropical jungle. About a half hour later, the tranquility of our trek was interrupted by shouts, sirens and gunshots. The MP's came plodding through ... "Why the hell did you leave the beach and the protected area? Don't you know that there are still headhunters here? Would you like your curly blonde head on a stake?"

Our biggest threat wasn't being in a war zone, apparently, it was encountering certain savage natives in the jungle.

MATS (Military Air Transport Services) flew us from base to base. They took out entire sections of seats and put in bunks so that we could sleep on flights between venues. At each stop, we'd do a show, visit/party with the boys and then board the plane for the next base, possibly a thousand miles away. It's always hard on the girls, because you've got to worry about how you're going to wash and do your hair, where you're going to get light and mirrors to do your makeup and all that girly stuff. Somehow, we managed through it all, even when we often performed on the back of flatbed trucks.

Greenland was amazing. We landed on a glacier. We were picked up in dog sleds and taken to our first stop, where the servicemen hadn't seen folks from home in months. This was a very small base at the top of the world. Our arrival was momentous, and the entire Eskimo community had been invited to the show.

We performed in a Quonset hut. The base crew built a riser for a stage and set up an organ, run by a vacuum cleaner motor, so that we would have music. These boys really did their best to accommodate us. I was the card girl that came out in the cute little tights for a fun opening. I would sing, dance and introduce all the other acts.

Well, I came out expecting a hut full of soldiers and lots of whistles. Instead, the first four or five rows were all Eskimo ladies. Some had babies nursing at bare breasts. "Showtime" took on a whole new meaning. I thought, 'Holy shit! They are not going to understand one thing I say.' But they nodded and smiled broadly.

Perhaps the most lasting impression of Greenland was my Christmas Eve on Thule Air Base. We had been to Midnight Mass held at the base auditorium / theater / chapel. The men's choir sang ... and it was beautiful. As we exited the Chapel, 140 degrees below zero, Christmas carols were being broadcast from speakers all over the base. We looked up at the most glorious display of Northern Lights in full ongoing, undulation. The sight and sound of this heavenly symphony brought tears to my eyes. As they rolled down, they froze on my cheeks ... to be expected at 140 below.

Joey Palk, Army Specialist – one charming, articulate, spokesman for the great benefits of U.C.L.A's Operation Mend

When my friends Debbie Reynolds, Connie Stevens, Ann Jillian, Ann Margret did some of their shows, they went into war zones. I was lucky. I got beautiful Pacific islands. However, I did see a lot of war causalities, especially in Hawaii. My several visit to Tripler Hospital really touched my heart. Some of the injuries were devastating. Lifting the spirits of the injured was most gratifying. This may have been the beginning of my reaching out to help wounded warriors everywhere.

Chapter 10

It was all Fun and Games!

 Game and talk shows were an important part of and asset to my career, and therefore my life. These shows introduced the real me to millions of Americans, who invited me into their homes. These television visits brought me many friends and fans ... friends who came to see me in stage appearances all around the country.

The Encyclopedia of Game Shows pictures *High Rollers* Alex Trebek and Ruta Lee on the cover. This show was produced by Heatter-Quigley, the creative duo also responsible for such shows as Hollywood Squares and PDQ. They agreed with co-producer Mary Markham's suggestion that I'd be a good cohost with Alex Trebek on *High Rollers.* Alex and I became good friends right away. First of all, we're both Canadian born, so there was a connection right off. He was new in town and I gladly shared my nifty friends, who became his long-term friends, as well.

When he married Elaine, pretty former Playboy Bunny, he adopted her little daughter Nicki. They bought a house in close-by Coldwater Canyon. We socialized often and were saddened when they divorced. However, their relationship remained friendly throughout life. In fact, Alex was the man who walked Elaine down the aisle to her new husband Peter Kares, a producer, with a great gift for building. With Elaine's great sense of style, the houses they buy and redo in West Hollywood have proven to be quite successful ventures. Elaine also has a great passion for art and even greater passion for animal causes.

Alex married again, to Jean, who is exquisite in every way. They have beautiful, now grown children. Alex's great assets were his loyalty and humor. Whenever I needed him, he came through for me, because he always considered us to be best buddies. He was unbelievably funny. Having had a Russian father, he knew accents and the comic idiosyncrasies of each nationality. He was also one hell of a good handyman. There wasn't anything that he couldn't build or repair. He had all the tools, as when our local hardware store was going out of business, he bought everything.

Alex had always been the "he could do it all man" and he proved it again. Now, as we go to print, he gave his pancreatic cancer a championship fight. He told me while he was a firm believer in an ultimate power, GOD, he was never taken by a formal religion...however he gratefully acknowledged that without the millions of daily prayers coming his way his valiant struggle would have ended long ago. Bravo, Alex, your generosity of spirit, wallet and loving attitude is a great life lesson to all.

My introduction to game shows began when I guested on Art Linkletter's House Party. A notice was sent to the drama department of LA City College. He needed a couple of college girls for a gag. It went well and I got invited back a couple of more times. That's where I discovered that I could work without a script. It gave me the courage to go on and do almost anything in front of millions of people LIVE without getting nervous and upset. Through the passing years, I socialized with Art. He was the first to ask my grandmother, whose release from Siberia made international headlines, to visit on his show. It was a touching segment.

Art touched hearts and tickled funny bones. He was substituting for Johnny Carson on The Tonight Show and I was a guest. I had just finished my leading lady role to Frank Sinatra and The Rat Pack in *Sergeants 3*. After the usual pleasantries, Art said, "Ruta you've just finished working with one of the most exciting performers in the world. Women adore him. Tell us, what does Frank Sinatra have that makes him so thrilling?" I said, "Well, Art, I can't put my finger on it right now."

There was a gasp and the audience started laughing. Art, who knew how to compound a laugh said, "Ruta, don't put your finger on it. Just tell us about it, which started a five-minute spontaneous laugh."

Art said, "We'd better go to Hugh Downs and a commercial." ... happened to be a live spot for the Hammond ORGAN Company. The laughter was nonstop. It wasn't just children who said the darndest things.

Mary Markham, who booked celebrities for most of the game and talk shows, took a real liking to me and had an amazing impact on my life. She saw that I was good at games, bringing a lot of bounce and energy to them. I did many shows for Mary, who became like a sister to me. She had to be tough to be in the business that she was in and this next story exemplifies that.

Mary had the sweetest mother, who lived with her in a beautiful apartment in West Hollywood. This four-bedroom apartment was also Mary's home office. She had worked solidly for three weeks, getting little sleep and was exhausted. Her mother was away for the weekend, giving her time for much needed rest. Anxious for undisturbed sleep, Mary unplugged all the phones, except for the hardline, which she covered with pillows in the hall closet outside of her bedroom.

To assure, much needed deep slumber, Mary took a sleeping pill. It was slow to work, so she took a second one and out she went. Something woke her and she was stunned to find a naked man standing next to her bed with an ice pick in his hand. Mary, a beautiful delicate blonde, was so pissed at being awakened, that she sat up and said, "Who the hell are you? You get out! Who invited you? Damn it! Get out! I didn't ask you to come in. Now put your clothes on and get the hell out that door."

The man sheepishly said, "I guess you don't want any tonight?" "No I don't want any and I will let you know when I do." He picked up his clothes and ran out. She sat there and suddenly realized what had occurred.

She heard the front door close and thought, 'Oh my God! How do I know that's he's not still in the hallway with the ice pick? How do I know he didn't just open and close the door to make me think that he left? If I lean out the window and yell, he's going to come roaring in here and stab me. Everybody's going to think it's just some drunk screaming anyway.'

She didn't know what to do, so she summoned up all of her courage and scurried down the hall to the telephone buried under the pillows. She pulled it on hardline cord into her room, slammed the door shut, holding it with her foot, because she was afraid if she leaned on it, the ice pick would come through the door and stab her.

She called the police. Investigators found the locks had been picked. The police psychiatrists later said that the fact that Mary was so hazy and didn't react out of fear, probably saved her life. Her angry admonishments must have reminded the intruder of "mother." Two weeks later in the same neighborhood, a girl was found stabbed to death with an ice pick.

Self-defense classes were suggested to all women. To my amazement, one of the experts was an 80-year-old woman, who taught how to deal with attackers or rapists. She said, "Ladies, you say, 'Alright mother fucker, show me what you can do'. Come on big boy. Show me." That usually would disarm the attacker because control and fear is their motivation. She said, "It's the hardest thing in the world to teach women to speak that way... to use abusive, awful, filthy language."

Thank God, Mary responded as strongly as she did. Eventually, she wed the love of her life, associate, Gary Damsker and it was a loving life-long marriage. In fact, I was Mary's bridesmaid/witness at their wedding.

Many wonderfully spent years later when Mary died Gary was totally distraught, as was I. My best and longest-term friend and mentor was gone. Gary was totally lost.

Ruta/Gary Damsker/Roni Miller. Gary and my beloved Mary sent me a new best friend

From somewhere …I assume heaven, Mary took pity on her anguished husband and provided a bright light in his life and thereby in mine as well. Enter Roni Miller, a precious new love for Gary and a new best friend for me. We clicked into a comfortable and loving relationship. We saw joyously a lot of the world together and helped each other through our miseries as well. With every daily prayer I thank my dearest Mary for being a best friend in the past and providing a me a best friend for the present and future.

I did a lot of shows for Mary and Gary, as a longtime regular on the original *Hollywood Squares* and several years as Alex Trebek's cohost on *High Rollers.* What a great time in my life! I was working on a successful show with a great company of people around me. It was also during that time that I began my successful marriage to Webb Lowe. I was swimming in happiness. Webb was then president of Bonanza Steak Houses a company based in Dallas, so therefor we bought and started our first home in that Texas city. This meant a weekly commute to "beautiful downtown Burbank" to tape *High Rollers* at NBC. I never ceased to be thrilled at having my picture on the studio wall, alongside Johnny Carson, Bob Hope and other stars of the NBC family.

Our High Rollers soundstage was next to *The Tonight Show and* every once in a while, I'd grab one of their guests, such as Lucille Ball, Ethel Merman, Buddy Hackett and bring them over to say hello to our studio audience. We'd roll cameras and they'd say, "Hi." to our national audience as well.

I got lots of mail commenting on my wardrobe, which was provided by Giorgio's of Beverly Hills. I got to show the clothes off to great advantage, with a very Loretta Young like entrance on every show. One time, on introduction, as cameras turned to me, announcer Kenny Williams said, "Here's Ruta Lee." I posed prettily. A beautiful crystal chandelier fell, hitting me on the head. I blacked out. When I came to, we tried it again. If I'm a little bit dippy, I can blame it on *High Rollers.*

George and Erin Pennacchio astonished me by
showing up on our flight to Lithuania... by the
way I am wearing one of her creations

While we're on the subject of *High Rollers,* George Pennacchio, ABC Television Entertainment Reporter, really made me laugh. He once owned a house in San Diego where he found some pictures the previous owner had left behind. That owner had once been a contestant on *High Rollers* and there was a picture of him in a Superman outfit that he wore on the show. I too was in that photo. I remembered him well. Ha, it turned out that he was the porn king of San Diego. George really laughed at that. Some weird people do show up as contestants on these game shows. They love you if they're winning and get really upset with you if they are not. In their mind, it's your fault.

By the way trivia tidbit - one day while I was thanking my pal George Pennacchio by saying "consider your ass kissed" he said, "Ruta if you ever write a book **that's** your title!" Another tidbit - George's lovely and talented wife, Erin, took over the task of creating my personal wardrobe... feathers, fringe, sequins and all. She is my Gown Girl.

I loved *Hollywood Squares*, *PDQ*, *Password*, *You Don't Say* and *Stump the Stars*. It was such fun to go to work, play games and get paid for it. Lucille Ball loved Stump the Stars because it was charades at it's best. Many of us would go over to Lucy's to play: Carol Burnett, Barbara Stuart, Dick Gautier and Carole Cook ... all- star games. It's surreal now when I think about it. How fortunate to be a member of Lucy's in-group. God I was so lucky!

I'm constantly being asked about *Hollywood Squares*. The most asked question is, "Were the answers ad lib or scripted? I can only tell you that standards and practices for NBC would not allow the questions to be seen in advance of taping. Producers gave us several words that were fail-safe if we went blank and had no answer. There was no way of knowing if these were ever used.

Hollywood Squares

I was once asked a question by host Peter Marshall relating to Dolly Parton's breast size. I answered, "Don't ask me. Peter, I have a tattoo on my chest that says, "In case of rape, this side up." That elicited roars from the audience and a frantic cut tape from standards and practices, until they decided whether it could air or not. The second most asked question is about the stars. Here's my take.

Paul Lynde: Venomously bitchy, but so funny it didn't matter.

Rosemarie: Brilliant on Dick Van Dyke and brilliant on Squares, an all-round good dame and still making us laugh thanks to reruns.

Wally Cox: One of the sweetest gentlemen I've ever known.

Charley Weaver: Delicious, countrified humor, sometimes delicious, "dirty old man."

George Gobel: A gift to early television and a delight to squares.

Abby Dalton: To this day, one of my favorite ladies.

Buddy Hackett: The wildest mouth and the biggest heart.

Host, Peter Marshall: A gifted Broadway Singer and actor, great guy and master extraordinaire of the three ring circus called Hollywood Squares.

One day on *Squares*, I wore a beautiful ring, a cabochon emerald, surrounded by diamonds. I took it off because it didn't go with the next show's outfit. I then did something incredibly stupid which I continue to do unfortunately, although not quite as often. I wrapped it in a piece of Kleenex and laid it down on my dressing room table. After the taping, I packed everything and threw all the excess tissues in the garbage. Driving home, I remembered. We never found that ring again.

Most all game shows taped a week of shows in one day. Three with a dinner break and then two more. The cast and crew all had dinner together. There would be a big community buffet. We just all had an especially good time. Wine was usually served, making the last two shows more sparkly.

Once on *PDQ,* hosted by my good buddy Dennis James, during one of these dinner breaks, I broke a front tooth, "Oh boy, what could I do?" We had two more shows to tape. We made a joke out of it. Dennis, the contestants, everyone involved including crew blacked out a front tooth. We looked like jack o 'lanterns and it worked very well.

Dinner break with Dick Gautier – Alex Trebek –
and Barbara Stewart Gautier

A few of the other game shows, you
might remember. . .

One of the earliest shows I did for Mary Markham was
Mike Stokey's **Stump the Stars, on CBS** which was the
newly revamped West Coast production of Pantomime
Quiz. Beverly Garland and I were the two regular girls and
some of the regular men were Sebastian Cabot, Richard
Long, Ross Martin, Stubby Kaye. It was the fastest paced
game show on television, taking quick thought and high

energy. It was great fun and even greater fun to get a check at the end of the week. Beverly was a super gal; her Hotels and reruns will keep her name around for a long time.

Name that Tune: "I can name that song in three notes," and often did. With today's rap music I would need the entire song and title too!

You Don't Say? **produced by Ralph Edwards,** was a fast-paced show with Tom Kennedy, who by the way was the brother of Jack Narz, both of whom were so important to the game show world. I discovered what a dummy I could be on that show because I had George and Muck and Bundy, but I couldn't piece the words together in the right order. I kept saying, George McBundy. As you know, the name was McGeorge Bundy, (presidential advisor to Kennedy) I knew I knew it, but I just couldn't make it work. I lost my contestant partner a lot of money.

I met two of my best boyfriends, Don Cook and Jerry Furlow on game show. They owned *AhMen* in West Hollywood. Their winner's prize was a Rosarita Mexican food party for 60. They put it to good use and held a Fiesta in the parking lot behind their store and sold lots of scanties. I don't remember the show, but I sure remember the party.

Regis Philbin – Ruta – President Ronald Reagan...the nicest and easiest man to interview

Chain Letter: I don't remember much about the game show itself. Host Jan Murray became a good friend. His beautiful wife, Toni, had been a showgirl at the Copa Cabana in New York where she met her comedian husband. They had a long and very good marriage. Unfortunately, Toni was injured in a freak accident in a parking lot, hit by a girl who didn't have a driver's license. Her injuries were so severe that 6 months later, she died. Jan's and my buddy, comedian Jack Carter was also severely injured, but survived and continued to bring his extraordinary comedy to the world until his death in 2015.

Password: Unforgettable Alan Ludden made every show a delight. A lot of fans were not aware that he and his remarkable wife, Betty White were musical stars, as well. They appeared in many venues across the country. And needless to say, Betty is still kicking butt today.

Tempo: with co-host Regis Philbin was like going to talk show boot camp, as it was 2 and half hours of live interviews and call-ins every day. This was my first job as an interviewer as opposed to interviewee. Regis had been going through a tough period. While we all now know that he was a great host/interviewer, he had at the time, just been fired from the *Joey Bishop Show.* OH, how time heals wounds, as he would eventually become America's prime host.

My first day on Tempo, Regis said, "You're going to do the interview coming up with a woman named Zelda Suplee. She was in from New York to talk about The Erickson Foundation, which in the early 60's helped transsexuals before, during and after surgery with their physical and emotional problems. I had studied the info-sheet and talking points. Zelda walked in, 5 by 5 in a British tweed-walking suit, Lisle cotton stockings, leather walking shoes and a Swiss fedora with feather. You get the picture.

She sat and proceeded to talk very seriously and informatively about problems transsexuals encounter. I was somewhat nervous as this was a subject never discussed on television during those times. I kept seeing Regis across the studio grinning at me like a Cheshire cat.

After some serious discussion, it was time for us to take phone calls, most of which were quite serious as well.

Several guys called in, one said, "No matter how much electrolysis I've had, I still get a five o'clock shadow. Another said, "my Adam's apple is too prominent". Ms. Suplee discussed many questions of this nature. Then a fellow called in and said, "This is all very interesting. I can understand how a man becomes a lady, but what happens when a lady wants to become a man?"

I then started hanging on to my chair. And Zelda said, "That's a very interesting question. I've just returned from Poland where I've witnessed the most amazing surgery." (I started to wet my pants, as Polish jokes were the fad then.) Zelda continued, "The donor who in this case is also the recipient, donates a rib creating the base of a penis. They also give the layer of fat and skin from the stomach area, which is wrapped around the rib. The surgeons then take the urethra, passing it through the penis they have constructed and attach it where it's needed. Now the female has a penis."

All I imagined was the donor used this large rib, not that little one. How I survived that first bizarre interview and kept my wits about me, I will never know. Transsexual surgeries are commonplace today. Christine Jorgensen was one of the first. She remains one of the nicest people I have ever met.

Dating Game: I saved this for last, because there's so much to tell and it's one of the best things that ever happened to me. I did the show many times. A guest star chose from 3 hidden contestants, one to go on a date, all arranged by the studio. Usually, I just took my appearance salary and never gave serious thought to going on the date. Who cared? That is until this particular date/show on which I was the guest star. Of the three men, two of them gave pleasant, mundane answers. The third was a snappy smart ass. I thought, 'Oh he's too full of himself, so I didn't pick him. Who did he turn out to be, but Las Vegas Comedic Star, Shecky Greene! I eventually went out with him a couple of times. He's a darling guy and so were his parents. Who knows, if we'd played our cards right, I might've been Mrs. Shecky Greene.

Anyway I wasn't going to take the prize trip, but then I listened to the itinerary. It was a trip to Tiger Tops in Nepal. Tiger Tops is a place like Tree Tops in Kenya, lodging built into the arms of massive trees. Included was an around the world trip on Pan American Airlines-first class. I thought, "If you don't take this trip Ruta, you're an ass." It was indeed one of the great treats of my life. On the way to Nepal, we stopped in Calcutta, India. People live, procreate and die in the streets there. Rats aren't killed. Cows are worshipped. The poverty is unbelievable, but still, India has great beauty and history. Agra, is the home of the Taj Mahal which I saw in the beauty of the moonlight, something I'd dreamed of doing since I'd first heard of the Taj Mahal. I went on my own that evening (Valentine's Day). My date and the chaperone chose dinner instead. Fools!

My experience was magical and moved me to tears. I screamed and shook in fear coming and going on the cab ride because of the snake charmers, all along the drive. Cobras! Yikes! I kept the windows rolled up in spite of the heat.

Our next stop, Nepal, was amazing. Kathmandu is a mystical city where the wisdom of the ages meets the cosmopolitan jet set. Most of the lifestyle here is meager. Nothing is wasted. I was fascinated by what appeared to be giant sized pizzas slapped on adobe walls, which turned out to be animal (mostly elephant) droppings collected from the roads and fields. They were formed into big patties, dried on the walls, then broken up and used as fuel. In the villages, chimneys were non-existent. They simply had holes in the roof (much like our American teepees).

International jet setters would fly in to have lunch with Boris Lizanovitch, who ran the Victoria Hotel, an incredibly old crumbling British relic. Boris was an especially interesting Russian. When the communists were taking over, he and his family literally walked across Russia, Siberia and then wound up in China. When he took the job in Nepal, managing the Victoria, some of the rich and famous came to see him because he was such an intriguing man. He had a beautiful luncheon for me with some of the local people and some jet setters who flew in.

His guest, a Prince of Nepal, took a fancy to me and invited me to the palace. I got a little nervous, thinking that I could wind up in a harem here. Nonetheless, a fascinating experience. Hmmmm... (I could've been Mrs. Her Highness Princess of Nepal.)

We then flew from Kathmandu to Tiger Tops in a DC-3, which most pilots will attest, is the best plane ever built. Our pilot was "Smiling Jack" in a turban. It was a stunningly beautiful flight between the Himalayas. Terraced mountainsides holding rice paddies with little villages carved and hanging off the sides of the mountain. It was amazing. Interesting to realize that the people on one mountainside probably trekked once in a lifetime, if that, to visit the other mountainside village.

Before we landed, our plane circled the field, which was the signal for the white robed villagers, waving big towels, to clear the cattle off the dirt strip runway. We were taken to our honest to God tree top hotel on elephant back. The walls were bamboo, the nights were cold, and the beds were warmed by copper vessels filled with hot coals.

The compound included a 50 square foot stockade, with a fence of pointed wood stakes, just like in the old Tarzan movies. The gate was pulled up and dropped by a rope. They tied down a young yak, about 1,000 lbs. It was bleating and didn't like being there. In came the tiger, much bigger than I expected. I've seen tigers in the zoo, but I'd never seen anything like this.

As he came in and the gate slammed down. He grabbed the yak, pulled it and the stake out of the ground and bolted over the fence that had to be at least seven feet high. Do you realize what kind of strength is in the muscles, neck, back and shoulders of that animal, to go over the fence, carrying that kind of weight? They didn't expect the tiger to bolt. They were planning to draw him in and release him. Being an animal lover, this was tough to witness. However, I have to accept nature's plan of one animal, feeding another hungry animal.

This Chitwan valley had been the Maharajas' hunting playground for many, many years. Thousands of beautiful tigers were killed. Tiger Tops was now a preservation sanctuary. I hope it still is.

My T.V. date was over. It was time to find some dates of my own. The people from the show were going back to Los Angeles. I was going to Israel. Boy did I have a time there. I met the minister of Industry, Zev Birger, who happened to be, like me, Lithuanian. His wife was a holocaust survivor, who had been a guinea pig in the camps. They experimented on her legs. She was so thankful when I gave her my then stylish go-go boots, which covered her bent, scarred legs. At this time, Jerusalem had just stopped being a divided city. I went to the Arab sector and had hummus for the first time. They served it on big pizza like trays, spread thin, drizzled with olive oil. You sopped it up with pita bread, yummy. Now, we always have it in our home.

Walking the streets of Jerusalem, Bethlehem and Nazareth was inspiring, as these were the same cobblestones that Jesus, Mary and the apostles had walked upon. The Israeli's have taken arid desert and turned it into beautiful, productive land of the proverbial milk and honey.

Next came Italy, I met a particularly exciting man, who showed me Rome to it's fullest. He was a pilot and I'm certain a gunrunner for the Israelis. He was so interesting that I was a little off schedule, meeting my girlfriend Erika Devore in Paris. (Erika, now Brunson) became an interior designer and is responsible for many of the palaces, houses and pied-à-terre of the Saudi Royal family. She is devoted to animal causes and has built and maintains Spay and Neuter Hospital Vans for low-income areas.

My travel people had arranged our Paris stay at the Plaza Athenee, a fabulously chic hotel. As I walked into our room, Erika, getting dolled up for a dinner date, asked, "Do you have any idea of what we're paying for this hotel?" "No, I assume it's a moderate amount." She said, "Well, it's not. It's $95.00 a day. " In the early sixties, that was a hell of a lot of money.

Then she said, "Don't order any food." She opened a deep drawer. There on a big tray was the Limoges breakfast service, left over croissants, honey and butter. "Eat that ... everything else is too expensive." So, in the morning, we decided to go hotel shopping for a lower rate: the Ritz, the Grande, the Meurice, etc. Picture this. Two little blonde tootsies, wrapped in their mink coats, asking to see what each hotel had to offer. That was fun.

We saw the best of Paris. We wound up in the Intercontinental, next door to the Ritz in one of those attic rooms with gabled windows, overlooking the rooftops of Paris. A beautiful double room, with a ballroom sized bathroom and only $29.00 a night. It was marvelous. I wish we could find that now.

We'd come in from a date, look at each other and say, "Are you hungry? I'm still hungry." We'd throw the mink coats over our jammies, jump in a cab and find a bistro to have onion soup, or escargot and a glass of wine. It was fun.

From there, we went to London, where once again, we had been set up with fabulous people to show us around. We met a man who was the editor for one of the fifteen daily newspapers. Any city that has that many dailies is a civilized city. He worked for a conservative newspaper and told us that he felt sorry for the Americans because they now would be the policemen of the world. The British had that responsibility for the last 100 years. He said, "You Americans are now going to be beaten over the head because you're going to do good things everywhere and everybody is going to resent you the same way the Brits have been resented."

He was so right. He showed the two snow queens, as he called us, the best of London and we had a hell of a good time. We will never forget him.

Another visit to London gave me a Royal moment. I joined friends for dinner at the extremely popular White

Elephant Restaurant. As I slid into my banquette seat, I bumped fannys with a delicate little lady. (seating was tight) As I apologized, I looked into beautiful blue eyes in a beautiful face. She laughed it off and only then did I recognize Princes Margaret. I guess you might say we dined together.

I think it was during my 6-week *Funny Bones* location in England when I ran into beautiful, funny lady Joan Rivers. Webb and I were strolling through London's Theatre District - Leicester Square when we came upon a theatre billboard for Joan's now playing show. We quickly purchased tickets and ducked into the matinee. She was brilliant! Tea, crumpets, cocktails and catch up conversation followed, ending only when Joanie had to get ready for the evening performance.

I look forward to every return to that great city, which I consider one of the best and friendliest cities in the world. As you can see folks, the game shows dealt me a winning hand in the game of life.

Chapter 11

From Siberia with Love

My life was good because my parents worked extremely hard to make it good. I think my entire generation has good lives because their immigrant parents worked hard and appreciated being in the land of the free. It's not just the Lithuanians, like me. It's Russians, Greeks, Poles, Armenians, Germans ... anybody who came to this country, recognized its blessings and thrived.

Those who remained in the old country suffered greatly through wars, famine and worse ... the onslaught of the red tide of Communism.

My grandparents had a small farm, which with hard work provided the family with food and sustenance. My mother, the eldest daughter walked barefoot across the fields to church, carrying her shoes, putting them on only as she entered the sanctuary. Those shoes had to be passed down to the next daughter.

Although extremely poor, my grandfather was highly respected in their little village. He was selected by the townspeople to be the arbiter in local disputes. He was considered fair, just and was the go-to man of the community. That's probably why he, his wife and children were among the first rounded up by the militia when the Red curse took Lithuania.

They were selected with others, no reason given and deported to Siberia in cattle cars, the same way the Jews were sent to the concentration camps. During the six-week winter trek, the men tried to keep the women warm, huddling them in the middle of the cars. At one of many stops, my grandfather, whose legs had frozen, was taken off the train. When they removed his boots, the flesh on his legs came off with them. Gangrene! He died. My grandmother didn't even know, as she was kept on the train that continued on.

Another deportee taken off the train along with my grandfather happened to be a Jewish acquaintance. When my grandfather died, his friend went to the rough burial site, made a cross for the grave and hung my grandfather's Rosary over it.

How ironic, many years earlier, my grandfather had been conscripted into the Russian army and was awarded medals by Lenin, which clearly now meant nothing, He was dead at the hands of the same communist party.

Real humanity comes into play under adverse conditions. That's when you see some people shine. That's also when you see more people that are unkind, cruel and will do anything to save their own ass. I grew up knowing that communism was a dreaded thing, but very few people my age, background, education and sophistication were aware of how insidious communism was and is.

Interesting side note: Many years earlier, my grandfather got a job in a Pennsylvania steel mill. He came over to the US alone, as my grandmother wanted him to get established in the United States. He wasn't happy here without his family, his farm and hearty peasant bread. (White bread just wasn't his loaf.) He went back to Lithuania; my grandmother never forgave him, but her dreams of America never diminished. I keep thinking about what she and my grandfather would have accomplished if he had stayed and brought one family member over after the other. Can you imagine what must have gone through his head on that cattle car deportation train? 'Why the hell did I leave the United States to come back to a poor farm and now the snows of Siberia?'

At the time of the deportations, my aunt, who lived close by my grandparents, saw the communist militia was there rounding them up. She grabbed her children and fled. Her husband had been with the Anti- Communist Partisans, (Whites), living and hiding out in the forests. The communists were the Reds. If you didn't join either team, they'd kill you. He had been with the Partisans. The communist militia found many of the Partisans in the woods and killed them all. They laid the bodies in the village square for identification. My aunt pinched the arms of her children and said, "If you see your father laid out on the road, don't recognize him. Don't scream. Don't cry. Don't do anything. We must survive." She saw him lying in the street. She didn't claim him. She didn't do anything. They hid out as best they could for a long time. Eventually they were found out and were also sent to Siberia.

When my grandmother got to her bleak Siberian destination, in the middle of nowhere, she found barracks with tin roofs, that housed 30 or so, with wood slat cots, no toilet, one stove for which they had to chop the wood themselves.

Sometime later she learned of my grandfather's death. She had no husband, no family, no food, nothing to live for. She went out on the felled logs on the river and wanted to drown. One of the prisoners caught her, "No, no Babushka, you mustn't do this." And he gave her his precious piece of bread. A Russian soldier/ guard took pity and made her the nanny of his two children, she became a beloved member of their family. Life was still hard for her, but she at least had a little food.

Years passed and the Russian family was quite sad to see her leave, when this old lady decided to hitch across Siberia, looking for other family members. Truck drivers hauling carpet, lumber and such across the snow and ice of Siberia, would give her a lift. Her perseverance paid off. She found loved ones and found comfort in the tiny hovel they had hand built and called home.

During all these years, my mother was diligently searching, through every relief agency, for her family as all communications had been severed during World War II. Finally, through the Red Cross, she located my grandmother and other deported relatives in Siberia.

In every family, in each generation, there's someone that takes responsibility and runs things. My mother was that one and passed the torch on to me. When, at age 16, I became a citizen of the United States, I was able to make application, "a Vyzov" to get my grandmother out of Siberia and bring her to the USA. A Vyzov was an invitation written in Russian, Lithuanian and English, hopefully currying favor with the Soviet authorities, Dear Grandmother, I would like to have you come and live with me in California. Due to your age and poor health, you will be a burden to your family and the state. I will take full financial responsibility for your travel and welfare...etc. etc.

Per the requirements of the Soviets, each of these invitations and accompanying translations had to be notarized. The notary seal had to be authenticated with the city seal, which had to be authenticated with the Sacramento State seal and then had to be authenticated with the U.S. State Department seal in Washington.

Those three sheets of paper grew with seals and ribbons to about a pound, which I then sent to my grandmother in Siberia. She would take it to the local commissar, who would examine the papers, be dazzled by the ribbons and seals, but inevitably said, "Nyet."

These invitations expired in 6 months, at which time I had to start all over again. This process went on for some **twelve years,** through different administrations, Nixon, Kennedy and I approached every politico I knew with my dilemma. I got sympathy from these heavyweights, but no action.

While I was becoming the hot new chick in Hollywood my mother was sending packages to Siberia and to whatever remaining family in Lithuania. Most of the family had been deported. Why? Nobody knows for sure, except that her youngest brother, who had been with the Anti-Communist Partisans was captured by the Reds and jailed where he died. Mother always lamented, "If only I'd gotten my little brother to Canada before the war halted immigration." Mom got her unmarried sister Malvina out in time, young Joseph would have been next.

The packages to Siberia were a lifeline. A total of 40 lbs. was permitted; one pound each of coffee, rice, chocolate and used clothes. My mother, God love her, would take apart jackets, roll up hundred-dollar bills and re- sew them into the seams.

All communication between us was censored. Letters arrived with deleted lines. We would write weeks later: "You know I sent you Joe's jacket, but mama it will be too big for you, so you could take out the shoulder pads. You know how to sew." We eventually found out that the money that made it through and was not confiscated by sensors, helped sustain their lives.

After Stalin's death, Siberian internments were somewhat relaxed and some families were permitted to go back to Lithuania, if they chose. A difficult choice, stay with what they had built or return home to nothing, as all their property had been confiscated and distributed amongst party members. Nevertheless, their hearts lead them home to Lithuania.

Back in Hollywood, I came home from the studio one day to find mother in a spate of tears. My grandmother never learned to read or write. My aunt wrote us, sending grandma's goodbyes etc. and thanks for everything we had sent, including her burial clothes (black skirt, white apron, white blouse and that traditional babushka scarf for her head). The doctor had told her she was going to die. I joined my mother in tears, my only remaining grandparent was dying. I had worked hard for twelve years on her behalf and now I'd never meet her.

I went out with friends that night for consolation. The more wine they poured, the more evident it became, that something dramatic needed to be done. Hell, I should call Khrushchev. So, I DID....at about two in the morning here in Hollywood, because that would be business hours in Moscow. Thank God, at the time, there were person-to-person calls, more expensive, but you didn't pay for the call unless you got through to your party. "Operator, I want to talk to Nikita Khrushchev, the Kremlin, Moscow, in the USSR." To my dismay, the American operator, asked, "How do you spell Khrushchev?"

It was hours and hours and hours of back-and-forth between me, the American and Russian operators: "No you can't," "Not available,", Not in," ... blah, blah, blah. By now I was sobering up and I was really headachy and not happy.

I didn't know if my grandmother was alive or dead at this point because it had taken weeks for her letter to arrive. Finally, the Russian operator called back and said, "Mr. Khrushchev, not speak English. You speak with Mr. Sukhodrev, the translator for Mr. Khrushchev?"

Aha, I remembered he was the good-looking translator, who traveled to the United States with the shoe banging Khrushchev. My father, who was fluent in Russian would laugh and say, "That's not what Khrushchev said." The translator had made his vehement remarks palatable for our Victorian ears.

"Yes, I'll speak to him." So Sukhodrev says, "Ms. Lee, we know all about you in the Soviet Union. We see your movies." I said, "Oh that's wonderful, I'm very happy to hear that. I would like to visit Lithuania; Soviet Union and I'd like to bring my mother and father."

He said, "Well why don't you talk to your Congressman about it?"

In frustration I said, "Jesus Christ! What has **my** Congressman got to do with my traveling in **your** country! It is not a matter of politics. It is a matter of the heart. I don't know if my grandmother is alive or dead. I want to go to Lithuania to find her or ... go to her funeral or graveside. "

At that time, Lithuania was a satellite country of the USSR. No outsiders were permitted in unless you were a very high-ranking party member.

So he said, "In thirty minutes, call the Russian embassy in Washington and present yourself again. I had already talked to the Russian Embassy ten times – everybody from the gardener to the dishwasher: "Nyet, nyet, nyet, nyet" was my only answer. So I thought "Oh, I'm getting brushed off again." Well, the hotlines between Moscow and DC must have been flashing, because this time my call was connected immediately to the first secretary of the embassy.

He was, to my surprise and relief, Lithuanian. Mr. Zenkevicius later became Lithuania's Foreign Minister and remained my very good friend. I'm fairly fluent in Lithuanian. Long story short, he told me to send all our documents to Washington and within 48 hours, we were on a Pan-AM flight to Lithuania.

It was the most incredible journey. At that time, you couldn't just fly directly into Lithuania. You had to go through a Soviet gate city, in this case, Moscow and then, double back a great distance to Vilnius, the capital of Lithuania.

Life Magazine was now following this adventure and why? Because before I left, I said to my publicist, Barbara Best, of Rogers & Cowan. "I'm going to the Soviet Union either to meet my grandmother or go to her gravesite."

And she said, "It might be a good idea for someone to know that you're going to the USSR, in case you don't get out. The state department had warned me: "Don't take your parents. You, Ruta, were not born there, so it's not likely they would detain you. They could however detain your Lithuanian born parents as primary citizens of the Soviet Union.

I said, "God is not going to be that unkind," so I risked taking them with me to Lithuania. They had not seen their families in 35 years.

Before I went on this mission, I had a quick lunch with James Bacon, top Hollywood reporter for the Associated Press. The story he filed with the wire service, captured international attention and made headlines worldwide. "Hollywood starlet goes to free grandmother from the Soviets." No wonder they were so nice to me in the Soviet Union. I had no idea of the international furor the press had raised as I was already en route to Lithuania and out of communication.

At that time, the beautiful domed churches of Moscow did not keep it from being unfriendly. The only friendly face was the Life Magazine photographer, who was assigned, much to my surprise, to cover the story. Once I got to Lithuania, things improved because I was the Lithuanian girl who made good in Hollywood. We were escorted/monitored everywhere. We found my grandmother had been moved from Klaipeda and the little tin topped and earth floor hut, that they lived in, to Kaunas, a big town. No doubt thanks to my international headlines she'd been miraculously moved by ambulance to a hospital, well intended but ill equipped. It was 1964 and they didn't even have aspirin.

Thirty-six painful years had elapsed since my mother and grandmother had seen each other. Knowing this, the entire loving hospital staff gathered around her room to see the Americans and witness the reunion. Everyone was in tears, except my grandmother who sat beaming her toothless smile. We were amazed at how well we were treated by the authorities, as I had made many anti-communist broadcasts for the Voice of America, which was banned in the Soviet Union. Communists running the country could not have been happy with my being there.

In retrospect, with the world watching, what else could they do? We had lunch with General Paleckis, then President of Lithuania. Even at a very young age, my politics were conservative, and the President said, "I know you don't appreciate my being a Communist. At least appreciate that I, a Lithuanian and a patriot am sitting in this chair and not some Chinese Communist." All the Baltic countries were being repatriated in an attempt to stamp out national pride.

The meager, joyless, unfulfilled life, forced on the people by this Godless system, cemented forever in my mind that Communism was doomed to fail. Ausros Vartai, (Gates of Dawn) was the only existing church in the capital city of Vilnius. The rest had been turned into museums. This church had the miraculous Black Madonna. Many miracles had been wrought by the Madonna. My mom, dad and I dropped to our knees at the shrine in gratitude for our miracle, finding my grandmother and gaining permission to bring her home to America.

Grandmother's health did not allow air travel at that time. Six months later, I returned alone to the USSR and started the red tape of her exit Visa. Final documents had to be obtained in Moscow. At the airport, leaving Vilnius, I asked my "bobute" (granny), who had never even seen a plane, if she was afraid to fly. She said, "The plane goes up, doesn't it? That's closer to heaven and God. Why should I be afraid?"

In Moscow, getting that exit Visa was another challenge. I was no big star there, nor did I speak Russian. We were booked in the Peking Hotel (then pride of Moscow). Granny and I would go down to the vast dining salon for meals, examine the large red velvet covered book of a menu to be told only 2 or 3 items were available. Potatoes, borsht and on some days, if lucky, caviar. Only options for breakfast, lunch and dinner. That was the Socialist/Communist version of a 5-star hotel.

The week there was bleak and Soviet bureaucracy icy. Our only ray of sunshine was the American Embassy, where bobute tasted and fell in love with her first American food, Campbell's Crèam of Mushroom soup.

After a tension filled week, with Soviet bureaucrats for clearances we were relieved to get on our once weekly BOAC flight to London--What a welcome change! Pretty stewardesses were working the aisles, serving champagne. Bobute leaned over and said, "No, no, no. Don't take anything. I don't have any money."

I said, "It's all taken care of. What do you want?"

My "Babushka" ready for her close-up

She beamed that toothless smile again and said, "Cognac." ... She'd heard about it all her life, but never experienced it. I thought she would sip it slowly through the entire flight to London. She downed it in one gulp and ordered several more, warming her heart and everything else.

Arriving in London, we found the world press had gathered to meet us, flashbulbs going off constantly through the impromptu press conference. Next morning, with breakfast came thirteen or more of London's daily papers. We were on the front page of every single one. My bobute looked at them and said, "Oh no! Ah, nice. No, no, not this one." When I said, "Why?"

She said, "In this one I'm smiling and you can see that I don't have teeth." At 92, she was fussing about a close up. Clearly, that's where my showbiz genes came from.

USA at last! After years of grueling hardships, Siberia, losing husband and children, her dream of America and freedom was fulfilled.

As we deplaned, bobute dropped to her knees on the Tarmac, kissed the ground ... and tearfully said, "Hallo AMERIKA! ACIU DIEVE!" (Thank you God!) I too, tear up when I think of that precious moment.

When she walked into my home, to her this was like a castle in a fairy tale. She took off her shoes, saying, "You can't walk on carpet." She'd only seen them hanging on walls, eastern European style To her, all modern conveniences were new and thrilling, even television was awesome. One day, my movie *Bullet for a Badman,* with Audie Murphy was on. Bobute was watching and screamed to my mother "Ruta's dead! Ruta's dead!" I had taken a bullet to the forehead. (See, good acting.)

Grandma visits Johnny Carson

I had guested on *The Tonight Show* many times. The show had followed my Soviet saga like the Perils of Pauline. When Johnny Carson brought the show to LA, he invited me to bring *bobute* for a guest appearance. She sat there rocking back and forth and smiling at Johnny, not understanding a word of English. Johnny nervously queried, "What is she thinking?" and she responded, "Tell him he is the sweetest flower that grows in the garden." You can imagine how the audience screamed with delight. Johnny humbly said, "That's the best compliment I've ever had."

I received thousands of letters, welcoming my grandmother to the United States – for which I will be forever grateful. Among them, a touching letter from Jerry Lewis, he said, "This was the most beautiful night of television, you and your grandmother"

Exactly two years, two months and two days later, I was guesting again on *The Tonight Show* in New York. The producer came to me with the sad news that grandma had died. "Will you be able to do the show?", he asked. "Of course, I'll go on, this show had helped bring her to this country. She had guested on it and tonight, millions of viewers can join me in a prayer for her, "Goodbye Amerika."

Though all the years that followed Lithuanian patriots of all ages put their lives in peril, striving to free their country of Communist rule and oppression. Unlike Eastern Europeans we Americans have never known or lived through deprivation of food, shelter, or cruelest of all, FREEDOM. After World War 2 the Russian Communist boot stomped down hard on the Baltic countries, however, resistance prevailed. After over 60 years March 11, 1990 was the day all Lithuanians had been fighting for... freedom at last.

The changes achieved in the ensuing years were astounding. The country rose from being a dark, dismal, miserable spot on the globe to a shining, joyful, living free nation. So much credit goes to those heroes who risked everything to attain independence, Vytautas Landsbergis heading the drive.

A few years later, Chicago resident, eminently successful business entrepreneur Valdas Adamkus (a prime example of achieving the American dream) gave his native Lithuania a great gift by running for and becoming President of Lithuania.

At Lithuanian White House – President Valdas Adamkus – his wife Alma – Ruta – Webb – Paula Kent Meehan

During his presidency I was invited to his newly restored White House. I was feted with a glorious all - star reception/ceremony and bestowal of Lithuania's highest civil honors for unstinting efforts for the beleaguered country. My farm bred relatives were truly dazzled to be in the celebrity filled White House...hell, so was I! This beautiful edifice was almost destroyed by the Russian troops billeted there for so many years.

My dear friend, Paula Kent Meehan flew in on her private plane for the event. She dashed to the hotel to change for our pre-event luncheon with President Adamkus and his lovely first lady Alma. Much to Paula's dismay she discovered she had not brought her Italian kid boots…so sneakers completed her haute couture outfit. Howard Hughes wasn't the only eccentric American.

This was an amazing year for me. Receiving my star on the Hollywood Walk of Fame and then Lithuania's highest honors filled me with gratitude to all those involved in making it all happen. Above all my loving friend Maryte Sepikas lead the campaigns like a Lithuanian Joan of Arc.

In 2019 I returned to Lithuania as principal speaker for The Women's Day Convention. During my visit I again spent precious time with the now former President and Alma and had the pleasure of meeting the soon to be elected new President Gitanas Nauseda. His smarts, style, grace and humor are reminiscent of his predecessor and mentor President Adamkus. I proudly state that both Ann Jillian and I, as newly confirmed citizens, voted for him. Bravo to him and all Lithuania.

Chapter 12

Principal Players

A question I get in every interview or with anyone that I meet on a plane, a bus or in a bank: "Who was your favorite leading man, the nicest, the nastiest?" I've shared stories about Frank and The Rat Pack, however, there were many other leading men I adored in both TV, movies and life. There were also many notable women, who were very much a part of my life. I've listed some of my work below with a small recollection about each.

The Twinkle in God's Eye – Movie: This film came immediately after my first, *Seven Brides*. The iconic Mickey Rooney and handsome Hugh O'Brien were the leading men. Also in the cast were Michael Landon, Mike Connors, all of whom became big stars and good buddies to me and more important *The Thalians*. In fact, Hugh O-Brian was our first Thalians president and Mickey Rooney was one of our last performing honorees.

Bullet for a Badman - Movie: Quiet, reclusive, American hero, Audie Murphy, was the star. But co-stars Darren McGavin, Alan Hale, George Tobias and Skip Homeier were such fun ... OMG, we laughed our way through this movie, shot in Utah.

My best buddy, Darren McGavin (Mike Hammer) and his wife Melanie, unbeknownst to me, made a down payment, on my behalf, thereby forcing me to buy my first house in Palm Springs, next door to them. In fact, he put in my sprinkler system for me. They did anything to keep me in their star-studded neighborhood.

Big warm teddy bear Alan Hale (Captain, Gilligan's Island) like most people didn't know that I tested for the role of Ginger. Of course, Tina Louise got the part. She had big tits, I didn't.

Marjorie Morningstar - Movie: This was the biggest book of the year and every girl in the world, except me, tested for the role that Natalie Wood got.

I played Gene Kelly's love interest, which was easy, as I was always in love with Gene Kelly, especially when he became our Thalians honoree. (Lucky me, being Natalie's size, I got to wear a lot of her wardrobe in the many Warner Brother's Television Shows I did.)

Man with a Camera - TV: Charles Bronson did several series before becoming an international superstar. He, like myself, was of Lithuanian descent, which established our ongoing friendship. He and his beautiful wife, Jill Ireland became very strong supporters and patrons of all Thalians events. Charlie also did a series called *The Travels of Jamie McPheeters*, costarring Kurt Russell. I danced in this one and loved working with Kurt.

Too bad he was only 12. Hmmm, I could've been Goldie Hawn, I mean Mrs. Kurt Russell.

Debbie - Charles Bronson, Movie icon and
good friend - Ruta

Yancy Derringer - TV: Jock Mahoney (Sally Field's
stepfather) was one of the nicest, most considerate
cowboy gentlemen in our business. If anybody had a
problem, Jock would be the first to help out.

I think he was also the only person to arrive at my black-tie dinner party at swanky Beverly Hills restaurant, La-Rue and instruct the valet on how to park his truck, filled with 1000 lbs. of horse manure ... his wife Maggie had the Lincoln that night.

Maverick - TV: I did many episodes. I couldn't help having a girlish crush on James Garner. He was adorable ... he was also married. The other Maverick, Jack Kelley was married as well. I could never have been Mrs. Maverick.

Gunsmoke - TV: Star Jim Arness was big brother to Peter Graves of Mission Impossible. (Side note – Jim was the giant carrot monster in one of the greatest sci-fi movies of all time, *The Thing.*) However, on *Gunsmoke,* he was a giant gentleman. I had the privilege of guest starring in several episodes in this timeless series.

One of the episodes will remain forever in my head and I had the bump to prove it. The scene called for the Marshall to enter my bedroom and throw a coy little seductress, me, over his shoulder and take me down the hall to Miss Kitty's Room. Big Jim did precisely what was called for and with me on his right shoulder, kicking and screaming, slung the curtain open with his left hand, thereby slamming my head against the doorframe. I went out like a light, no longer kicking and screaming. The next thing I knew, I was lying on the floor, big Jim hovering over me, tears rolling down his cheeks, saying, "Oh thank God I didn't kill you." It was a unique, wonderful and interesting way to come to.

James Arness – he knocked me out in more
ways than one

The Line Up - TV: Warner Anderson and Tom Tully
starred in this first San Francisco based series. Producer,
Jaime Del Valle liked my work and hired me often through
the show's five-year run. Thanks to him I got to play
dozens of different characters from debutantes to
drugged out hookers. He was also a film and radio

producer who was married to Virginia Gregg, one of radio's foremost leading voices.

He would generously allow me to bring my mother to San Francisco. Thanks to Jaime I got to know and fall in love with the city. He was the kind of guy that had he been single, I would have been extremely interested in I think. He had that quiet kind of power, which I found incredibly attractive. His family held big California land grants. I think they owned most of the San Fernando Valley, at least the part that Bob Hope didn't. Jaime called one day and said, "How's your tennis game?" Not knowing what he had in mind, I mumbled, "Ok." He said, "Great, we have a role for you starting Monday. You're a tennis player at a San Francisco Country Club." I panicked. I had never played tennis, so I called upon tennis champ, Tony Trabert and begged him to spend that weekend teaching a novice to play. Monday in San Francisco when I got the script, it read, the ball comes to Peggy. She attempts to hit it and falls flat on her face. I'd spent two days learning how to play tennis only to find out that I didn't have to. Oh well, at least I looked cute in the tennis outfit.

Tab Hunter Show - TV: I loved Tab then and I love him now...never physically. He's of a different persuasion. But he's been a beautiful, joyful friend through the years.

Werner Klemperer – Much more handsome
here than as Colonel Klink in Hogan's Heroes

Operation Eichmann - Movie: I played Werner
Klemperer's (Eichmann) mistress in this movie, the first,
when run on television to get TV residuals. It showed
Russians as the good guys and Nazis as the bad guys. This
film ran continuously in the Soviet Union, which didn't
hurt when I went to get my grandmother. Werner's
father was the internationally celebrated conductor Otto

Klemperer. Werner had a super long run, on Hogan's Heroes. The many times I guest starred our reunions were always joyous. He was a most informed and interesting companion.

Bat Masterson and Burke's Law - TV: I loved Gene Barry, who also was of Lithuanian descent. He could do it all: a Broadway singer, dancer, (La Cage aux Folles) cowboy star and gentleman detective. He and his wife were my Palm Springs cronies.

Hootenanny Hoot - Movie: Peter Breck, Johnny Cash, directed by Gene Nelson, one of the great Hollywood dancers turned director. He became a good friend. He and his wife often stayed with me in Palm Springs. His widow Jean is one of my dear generous friends. I fly up to San Francisco several times a year to visit my 95 year old friend. She herself was a dance star in her youth. She underwrote a Thalians Ball in tribute to Gene. Who knew that Cash would become an American icon...I guess his wife June did?

Johnny Staccato - TV: John Cassavetes was one of the foremost Actors Studio people to make good in Hollywood both on the screen and behind the camera. He was married to the brilliant Gena Rowland, with whom I have maintained a Hollywood friendship, an actress too divine for words. My big regret is that I never got to work with John as a director.

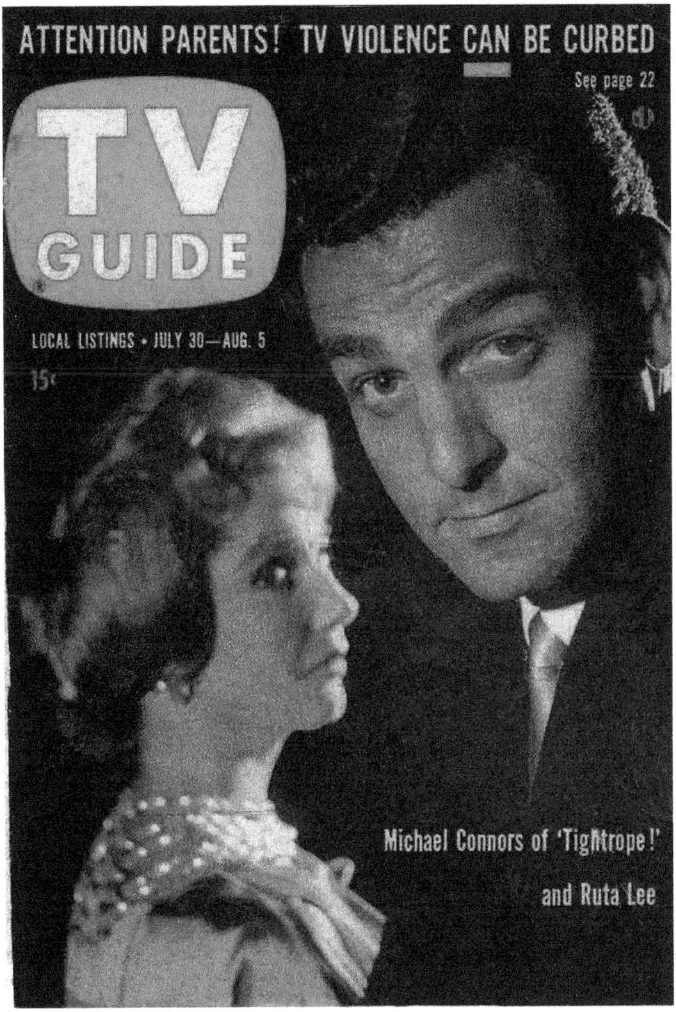
ATTENTION PARENTS! TV VIOLENCE CAN BE CURBED
See page 22
TV GUIDE
LOCAL LISTINGS • JULY 30—AUG. 5
15¢
Michael Connors of 'Tightrope!'
and Ruta Lee

Cover of TV Guide

Tight Rope/Mannix-TV: Mike Connors, known as Touch during his basketball days under UCLA's John Wooden is one of those handsome Hollywood men I truly admire, he was happily married to Mary Lou, since 1949. I first met him on *Twinkle In God's Eye* (with Mickey Rooney).

Harrigan and Son - TV: Pat O'Brien was the most beloved actor in America. When he came to my wedding, I felt like I had the whole Irish Catholic community there because of his joyous persona. He toasted with these words, "May the road rise to meet you. May the wind always be at your back. May the sun shine warm upon your face. May the rains fall softly upon your fields. And may you get to heaven a half hour before the devil knows you're dead."

While his series was short-lived, he has remained one of the foremost actors of his generation. I'm honored to have known and worked with him.

Stagecoach West - TV: Wayne Rogers, a good actor, very savvy financially. I followed him on Fox Finance Report and listened to his tips on stocks and bonds. However, I rarely buy stocks only bonds.

Outlaws -TV Australian Rod Taylor, also a big film star, was another Palm Springs buddy. He was also a close friend of my *Talk of the Town* co-host Toni Holt Kramer. Rod unfortunately was a very heavy drinker. I loved him dearly… up until his 4th martini.

Dick Powell Theater, Starsky and Hutch, Fantasy Island, Love Boat, Mod Squad and too many others to name – TV: Texas born, Aaron Spelling was a mediocre actor, turned wildly successful producer, who dramatically influenced our industry. His work defined pop culture for many years. I talk a lot about leading men, however, it's also producers like Aaron who helped shape my career. Aaron produced so many shows that I worked on. When I first met him, he was married to Carolyn Jones; both of them thin as rails. I met him at their house in the valley before he was THE Aaron Spelling. New York comedian, turned successful producer, Jimmy "You've gotta have Heart" Komack often stayed with the Spellings, claimed their intimate moments sounded like two skeletons banging on a tin roof. We were all Palm Springs neighbors and hung out together on weekends. I remember the time he hired me for a *Mod Squad* episode. I was due in makeup at 6 am. As luck would have it, the night before I contracted one of those 24-hour bugs and spent the night with my head in the toilet. I called in sick to the studio that morning; they had 25 minutes to replace me.

Later that night I felt great and I didn't want to miss the party at Sammy Davis Jr.'s. Who was there but Aaron Spelling? He looked at me and said, "I thought you were sick?" I said, "This morning I was. Do you think that I would turn down a job and money? Come on Aaron!" I'm not sure he was convinced, but he still cast me many times after that. It was always a pleasure to work with the gang on his *Love Boat*.

In fact, Captain Gavin McLeod is a great song and dance man. We worked together on "Grossingers," a Broadway bound musical that didn't make it past Texas.

Gavin McLeod – Grossinger's – I didn't know
he was such a great song and dance man

Gaby - MGM Film - I returned to MGM when cast in
Gaby, yet another remake of Waterloo Bridge. This one
starred Leslie Caron and John Kerr, replacing the
previous stars, Vivien Leigh and Robert Taylor.
Charming old-time director Curtis Bernhardt   had

insisted on beautiful authentic sets filled with fine furnishings. It astounded me how poorly the crew and cast treated the priceless antique furniture, some of which, by the way, when auctioned, Debbie Reynolds bought for her valuable collection.

Bonanza - TV: Lorne Greene was a fellow Canadian and one of my favorite actors. Mike Landon was in my life for a lot of years and left us way too soon. Mike was a young Renaissance man. He wrote, produced, directed and acted. While we did many shows together in our early years, as a producer, he never hired me. Hmmm... Maybe it was because I was so friendly with my Palm Springs neighbor, his ex-wife Dodie.

Speaking of Bonanza, the man I slept with, my husband Webb Lowe, was formerly president of the Bonanza steak house chain. The TV Stars were tied into marketing the restaurant.

Rawhide - TV: This was Clint Eastwood's first series, and the rest is movie history, accomplished actor, director, producer, musician and friend for 50 years. He hasn't hired me either. Hmmm... although I was married to him...at least on TV! My first of several guest appearances on Rawhide initiated occasionally dating its good-looking co-star Eric Flemming. That handsome face we all knew, had been rebuilt after being shattered by a steel girder. He was gorgeous, great voice, beautiful body, tall and lean, a great sexiness about him. Sometime later, he was shooting a film in South America with actor Nico Minardos when their dugout canoe overturned in the river. Nico swam to safety, but Eric was swept away by the current and assumed drowned. Nico told me it was Piranhas.

Clint Eastwood...and I even got paid for this

Both Clint and Eric were adept gun handlers and we often took part in the Quick Draw contests in Vegas , sponsored by Colt Firearms.   Many Western stars participated. I cherish the beautiful pair of nickel plated Six Shooters that Colt Firearms president Fred Roff awarded me. Along with horsemanship western cowboys and wranglers taught me how to respect and handle guns. Thanks y'all.

Gun Hawk Poster

The Gun Hawk - Movie: Rory Calhoun was one of the many clients of infamous Henry Willson, the gay powerhouse agent with a huge roster of stars, some gay, some straight. For me, working with Rory was a dream come true. When I grew up in Montreal, you had to be sixteen to go to the movies. My mother would doll me up, lipstick, one of her fur coats and I, at 10 or 11 acted 16 and got away with it.

One of the few movies I got to see was *Adventure Island* with Rory. He was so gorgeous he was my dreamboat. To think, years later in Gun Hawk, being leading lady to him and Western star Rod Cameron was truly living a dream. Rory, his wife Lita Barron and I, remained dear friends for a long time.

Arrest and Trial - TV: Ben Gazzara and Chuck Connors were two leading men that were easy to admire. Ben was an Actors Studio person that made a big splash on Broadway and in films. I later worked with him on the miniseries, *People Like Us.* Chuck "Rifleman" Connors was an all-around good guy. I loved them both.

Wagon Train - TV: Ward Bond. Just like he always played...a true man's man. I met Bob Fuller of *Laramie,* later of *Emergency* when we both guested on this show. He was one of a few actors that I dated, mostly for publicity purposes, no romance, but great friendship. He and his wife now live in Texas, but we happily meet up at Western Film Festivals.

Twilight Zone – TV: It's one of my most cherished TV roles and indelible to my fans. Sexy little bitches are such fun to play. My costar, Patrick O'Neal was a wonderful, always working actor. I was also crazy about creator Rod Serling. I loved everything about Rod except his smoking, which eventually caused his untimely death.

My favorite episode of Twilight Zone with
Patrick O'Neal

He left us far too young and we lost a huge talent. Take a look at any movie made before the 80's and everybody was smoking all through the movie. It's a great actor's prop. I'm surprised that I never took up smoking, as there is a lot of sitting and waiting while shots are set up. Thank God I never picked up the habit.

77 Sunset Strip - TV: Efrem Zimbalist Jr. was the epitome of a gorgeous sophisticated, leading man. His father was a world-famous violinist. Efrem was also a highly moral man, a good solid Christian who did a lot within his church. He was devoted to "Feed The Children," and "Childhelp," among many other charities. He was my idea of an ideal man. I also worked with his lovely daughter Stephanie on several productions.

Handsome Roger Smith, married to beautiful Ann Margret, was the costar along with Ed "Cookie" Byrnes. I enjoyed my many visits to *77 Sunset Strip,* both film and the real restaurant. Trivia Tidbit... My best friend, Paula Kent (Meehan played the hatcheck girl in the series. That was before she founded RedKen Hair care products, a multimillion-dollar company. That's better than checking hats.

The Virginian - TV: Jim Drury has been a lifetime pal. We met early in our careers on *Walter Winchell Files.* I guest starred several times on *The Virginian.* Jim is a staunch conservative and campaigned several times for candidates of like minds. On one of the Ronald Reagan airplane jaunts to smaller communities in northern California, we wound up in Eureka. We had to stay overnight after attending another rubber chicken dinner, which neither of us ate.

We were too busy campaigning. Reception over, we were still hungry. Gentleman Jim said I'll buy you a hamburger. However, at this hour, everything was closed. We gave up and so I went back to the motel and went to sleep. Some hours later, I was awakened by Gentleman Jim, knocking on my door. He had brought me sustenance. Seems that he had driven around the county, looking for a diner and in the process, pulled up to the security gate at a local prison. The guard, duly impressed that The Virginian was at the gate, called the warden, who invited Jim to his house. The warden, after hearing of Jim's mission called upon a trusty to prepare some sandwiches. This was the gift that Jim came bearing. I've eaten many peanut butter and banana sandwiches, but never before prepared by inmates doing hard time.

Our candidate, Ronald Reagan won, great years for the U.S.A. Jim and his wife now live in Houston. I am always delighted to see him and share some laughs at Western Film Roundups and most recently during his tribute, at the unique Gene Autry museum in Hollywood. Gene and his wife became friends and supporters of my Thalians. I am proud to claim his widow Jackie as one of my closest Palm Springs pals.

The Bill Dana Show - TV: I brought my 95-year-old Lithuanian grandmother to the set when we were filming this show. It was the first time that she'd ever seen movie making. Bill is one of the dearest people God ever put on this earth. He is a true astronaut fan and they love him. He lives in Hawaii but flew in at his own expense to join *The Thalians* when we honored the fourteen original astronauts.

Gomer Pyle U.S.M.C. - TV: My darling Jim Nabors and I have many mutual friends. When I got my star in

Hollywood, he sent a message and orchids from Hawaii. He's just an all-around good guy. A few years ago, a group of us including Debbie Reynolds spent New-Years at Jim's home in Hawaii. What a host! Enthusiastic about everything! He loves to laugh and carry on. I adore Jim and along with the country, prayed hard for him when he was five days from death. God must have listened because he got a kidney which kept him going for many years. He continued his many charitable activities with special emphasis on transplant surgery till he died, leaving us with a hole in our hearts and humor.

Wackiest Ship in the Army - TV: Handsome Gary Collins, later married Miss America, beautiful Mary Ann Mobley. Both were my good buddies.

One of the funniest work experiences I ever had was on the back lot of Columbia Ranch, where the Wackiest Ship was anchored in a big lake. After a long hard day of shooting the last scene called for the entire cast, including me, Gary and costar Jack Warden to jump into a skiff and row rapidly across the lake to the wackiest ship, dodging enemy bullets. This was a costly set up. A camera on the hill for the long shot, a camera halfway down for the medium shot and one on the beach for a close-up, all to roll simultaneously at the director's signal. The sun was setting. We were losing light fast. The director yelled, "Action. All cameras rolling." We all got aboard. Gary starts rowing furiously. About halfway the boat started sinking, as did the sun. The cast was now waist deep in water, laughing so hard, we peed. All we could hear from our totally frustrated, director Dick Sarafian was, "Ah shit, I quit." (And he did. He directed only this episode.)

The laughs with Gary continued, especially when we shared the stage for several years in the Palm Springs musical review, *Senior Class*. His beautiful Mary Ann was also a member of the cast. Unfortunately, handsome Gary had some alcohol related problems and left us far too early. After a long struggle, cancer claimed my dear friend Mary Ann.

Andy Griffith - TV: Andy was one of the most fun human beings. He made everything a lark. I also adored Don Knotts. The two of them were so funny together. Andy had warmth and humor about himself and his country ways. For a guy who had been on Broadway, starred in movies, his humility was refreshing. We played very well together. In one of the episodes, I snowed Barney, as a reporter, pretending to be a college girl. In another episode I played a movie star Andy visits in Hollywood.

When the show changed title to **Mayberry RFD**, I did a few more episodes with Ken Berry. Ken was a wonderful dancer, who got to really strut his stuff on *The Carol Burnett Show and Mama's Family*.

The staying power of all the shows is amazing as they are still played day after day, year after year. Thousands of fans gather annually in Mt. Airy, North Carolina to celebrate Mayberry Days with all its *television residents*.

I regret that I didn't spend more time with little Opie ... who grew up to be famous director, Ron Howard. He might have remembered me fondly for one of his movies. The little shit hasn't hired me yet.

Judd for the Defense - Movie: Carl Betts was divine. Sadly, he died too young. I played a news reporter. On this show I met actor/artist/ director Tom Troupe, who played a deaf mute ... outstandingly! He and his multitalented wife, Carole Cook, Lucy's protégé, are my forever friends.

Tom hand makes the most intricate greeting cards, which they send for special occasions. He calls making them, *therapy*. I call them *love*.

At one of the many benefits, Carole came out on stage in a lovely black gown weighed down with jewels to her knees. She said, "I'm so happy to be here. I realize that I'm sort of overstated with my beautiful diamonds, but I didn't want to leave them in the safe at Motel 6." Great line! Great broad!!

Wild Wild West - TV: Bob Conrad was gorgeous and extremely athletic, but co-star Ross Martin really knocked my socks off. He was not only an amazing raconteur, but a great actor who could easily play good guys or murderers. I was happy to have guest starred on many episodes. On one of them, we were a traveling circus with elephants, goats, monkeys, etc. Being an animal lover, it was heaven. In later years Bob had a radio show on which I have guested. He had some difficult health issues not easy for this fabulous athlete. No wonder he often got testy.

Memphis, "Gathering of Guns," Western stars
of film and television – how many can you
name?

Perry Mason/Ironsides - TV: Handsome, Raymond
Burr always wanted to be a leading man, but he had an
ongoing weight problem. I was crazy about him. He had
the most gorgeous eyes and longer lashes than mine.
Ray was one of the people in our industry who was
under the radar about his sexuality. Nobody talked
about his preference. It was quiet Hollywood
knowledge that he was gay. His constant female
companion, the lovely Evelyn Russell, was a lesbian.
The show's producer Gayle Patrick Jackson took me
under her wing and cast me in many different roles. She

was a big film star in the 30's and 40's. This was a woman that I couldn't refer to as a girlfriend because she was quite a bit my senior, but she was certainly a friend to me. She and her husband, Cornwall Jackson, included me in their sophisticated dinner parties. This beautiful lady, one of the first female producers, didn't mind having pretty young things around. She was secure in who and what she was. I am eternally grateful for the many shows and many roles she let me play.

Barbara Hale was a lovely lady and a great jokester. She and Ray were constantly playing pranks on each other. I was honored to speak at her funeral. I also had the pleasure of working with Ray on *Ironsides*. Wow, he had a long and wonderful career, deservedly so.

The Flying Nun - TV: It was a delight to work with Sally Field. Her stepdad was my dear friend, Jock Mahoney (Yancy Derringer. On her show I played a nun with the longest damn eyelashes you've ever seen, batting them at my costar Dick Gautier. Later, Sally was our Thalians Ms. Wonderful honoree. She did a mental health promotional film for us that we still use to this day.

Love American Style - TV: I did probably a half dozen of these shows with lots of different leading men: Regis Philbin, Jack Carter and Rodney Dangerfield. Once again, I worked with Dick Gautier who happened to be married to my best friend actress Barbara Stuart. She was also up for the same role of Dick's wife. I got it. They said she wasn't right for the part. Hmmm, reminds me of the time I went in to see Garry Marshall about a part. The script literally called for a Ruta Lee type. I didn't get the part. Garry said I was too on the nose.

Marcus Welby MD - TV: What a thrill it was to work with an icon like Robert Young and (be still my heart) James Brolin. The show's costume designer, Grady Hunt, put me in fabulous wardrobe. He also designed and costumed all my future musical stage productions.

Howling in the Woods - Movie: After *I Dream of Genie*, Larry Hagman and Barbara Eden teamed up again for this movie shot up in Lake Tahoe. I'm happy Barbara continues to be in my life. She will appear for *The Thalians* whenever asked and continues to be a loving, giving girl. Larry Hagman was the son of my favorite musical comedy star Mary Martin.

Hogan's Heroes - TV: I had great fun with Bob Crane, Werner Klemperer, Robert Clary and all the crazy POWs. The cast was made up of wonderfully funny people, making it difficult to control laughs on the set. I played a lot of different nationalities and hence accents. Bob's bizarre murder left us very sad. Drugs, sex, irresponsible behavior and his murder sadly ended a brilliant career.

Indict and Convict: George Grizzard, Eli Wallach, Harry Guardino were all important New York actors who came to television. I was proud to work with them. Also a treat, was spending time with guest star, Myrna Loy. All Americans fell in love with her in the *Thin Man* movies, as the Mrs. of Nick Charles ... played by William

Powell, who with his real wife Mousie were my neighbors in Palm Springs.

Doomsday Machine - Movie: This was a piece of shit with a great cast ... Dennis Miller (Tarzan) also became the Gorton's fisherman ...Oscar nominee, Mala Powers (Roxanne in *Cyrano de Bergerac*) ... Bobby Van, one of the great dancers of our time and the legendary Henry Wilcoxon, (*Ten Commandments, Cleopatra*), a huge star in the 30's, 40's and 50's. He was the son- in-law to Cecil B. DeMille He belonged to the Screen Directors Guild. He would invite me to their screenings. Occasionally, we would have dinner and drinks, as he loved having a cute young lady around. I really admired him, but it was a lovely nonromantic, May-December relationship. I appreciated the time I spent with icons and he was certainly an *icon.*

Roll Freddie Roll - Movie: Tim Conway starred. I played wife to comedian Jan Murray. Beloved, funny man Tim remained a friend until his passing. His son, Tim Jr. has a very popular Los Angeles radio show on KFI. Not long ago I interviewed them both for Lifestyles TV. Tim has done many Thalians shows for us. He was one of the most delightful and generous people on the face of this earth. Nobody but nobody has made me laugh as hard as Tim Conway on *The Carol Burnett Show*. My favorite sketch ... the dentist who accidentally keeps injecting all parts of his body with Novocain. We could all take lessons on comedy timing from Tim Conway and maybe some lessons on living life, as well. He was such a genuine, good, human being.

Tim Conway – humorist and humanitarian

Mork and Mindy - TV: Robin Williams was so frenetic, so crazed, but soooo amazing. His genius was apparent on this series. Darling Pam Dawber was in the cast. She was and still is adorable. Years later, when we were honoring Whoopi Goldberg at *The Thalians*, Robin flew in from Napa to do the show and of course as always brought down the house. I really tried but he was most reticent about becoming our honoree in spite of being most deserving of our award.

He supported so many worthy causes with his time and talent, which in his case was more valuable than money. I think you will all agree that in our business Robin was fearless and peerless. I must mention that my best friends Margie and Bob Petersen sent their plane to transport Robin. They too were peerless in charity.

The Ghosts of Buxley Hall - Movie: This was a Disney film, a wonderful reunion with Vito Scotti (*The Flying Nun*). We played a Count and NO-ACCountess. For the first time I experienced the vaudeville schtick of pie in the face. Loved it!

Threes Company - TV: John Ritter (also a Hollywood High Grad) was so sweet and died so young. This has remained a very big show that is still on the air everywhere. The casting director, David Graham became a close friend. Beautiful Suzanne Somers is a far cry from the ditzy Crissy she played on the show ... author, entertainer, businesswoman and health advocate is my Palm Springs neighbor and friend.

Simon and Simon - TV: Parker Stephenson was the cutest guy. He and Kirstie Alley (Cheers) married and moved to Maine, where they did not live happily ever after. Gerald McRaney, whom I like very much, is outspokenly conservative. In our business that's dangerous if you want to keep working. He has been married to my darling Delta Burke for many years and has been her rock, giving wonderful support emotionally and physically.

Rooster, Spurs of Death - Movie: Another non-memorable film. Moneyman/producer, Gene Bicknell cast himself in the lead role. He made his money in the garbage bag business and frankly that's where that film belonged. Gene's acting ability did not live up to his astute business abilities. Gorgeous, Ty Hardin was the other leading man. I had worked with Ty on his Warner Brothers TV series *Bronco.* In fact, I partnered with him in his screen test for the part. The other man in Rooster was a young Vince Van Patton, who played my son. Look how small the world is. His real parents, the Dick Van Pattons became close friends.

Madame's Place - TV: Waylon Flowers was a most unusual leading man because he was a Madame. His girls/puppets were very, very bawdy. The language and double entendre seemed to be overlooked by network standards and practices. Puppets can say what people can't and hell it was funny.

Chips - TV: Handsome Eric Estrada. After CHIPS he became a huge star on Mexican Telenovelas. He also became a law enforcement officer, who has travelled the country talking to kids about law, order and responsibility. His wife, Nanette and he have a beautiful daughter and we've shared many travels together. Good people, good friends.

Fantasy Island - TV: Star, Ricardo Montalban was married to Georgiana, my friend Loretta Young's sister. Long before I met him, I'd see them all at Saint Victor's Church (which I promptly renamed our Lady of Loretta). Oh, what beautiful people! I first met Ricardo when Chrysler donated a car to *The Thalians* for auction. He was the company spokesman and came to present the lucky winner with keys to the LeBaron, Corinthian leather and all. For many years, he also joined Edward G. Robinson, Agnes Moorhead and Ed Begley Sr. in *The Thalians Quartet* ... unforgettable comedy readings by this iconic group. On my several guest-starring visits to Fantasy Island, I found Ricardo was the loveliest gentleman ... so suave and so charming. As a leading man, he really knocked my socks off.

Herve (De Plane, De Plane) Villechaize tried, but he didn't knock anything off, nothing to do with his size (I adored Billy Barty). Villechaize was just a putz. Adorable, Oscar nominee, Terry Moore and I finally worked together after years of friendship which continues to this day.

The Rousters - TV: Chad Everett, Hoyt Axton and Jim Varney ... Jim was comedically brilliant and died far too young, as did country star Hoyt Axton ... both neat guys. Chad was adorable, good looking, in one series after another, a great friend to *The Thalians*. He also died way too young.

First and Ten - TV: A football series, starring Delta Burke. I found her to be beautiful, interesting and a touch insecure. Hell, what did she have to be insecure about? She was a beauty queen with talent. The leading men were all big brawny football players, hands like ham hocks, but gentle as lambs. The principle leading man was OJ Simpson ... we don't apply gentle lamb to him!

Delta - TV: Delta Burke. This came sometime after First and Ten. I met the incredibly talented Beth Grant (Sordid Lives) on this. We did *Steel Magnolias* together for Garry Marshall's Falcon Theater. Earl Holliman, from Policewoman, was the leading man on Delta. Earl is also a leading man in every animal's life. He's the former president of Actors and Others for Animals, a role Jo Anne Worley has taken, who by the way is one of the truly gifted and good people on this planet. I'm proud to have her as my friend.

Benson - TV: Robert Guillaume, a pleasure to work with ... a good comedy actor and a fine musical performer as was Inga Swenson; 110 in the Shade on Broadway. For me, it was fun playing a psychic on a showroom stage location in Vegas.

Hotel - TV: Connie Sellecca, James Brolin. I always thought he was one of the cutest guys in the world. When he divorced there was hope for us single girls, but then Barbra got him. I later, again, worked with the delightful Connie in *People Like Us.*

People Like US - Movie: ... also starring Dennis Farina, Eva Marie Saint and Ben Gazzara, which made it a lot of fun. Sometime later, I was so happy to see Dennis, formerly a real-life Chicago cop, on my favorite show, *Law and Order.* His death is a real loss. (Side note: *People Like Us* was written by Dominick Dunn. His daughter was murdered by her boyfriend, adding to the bizarre series of deaths of many actors associated with the *Poltergeist* movies.)

Coming of Age - TV: Produced by Barry Kemp and Emily Marshall (Mrs. Doc Serverinsen) with Paul Dooley, Phyllis Newman, Glynis Johns, Alan Young and me. We all grew up with Alan on Mr. Ed. He was a dear and funny guy and I was lucky enough to have him as a leading man in Sacramento in *Best Little Whore House in Texas.* Having seen *A Little Night Music*, it was great pleasure to have time with iconic British actress Glynis Johns, who introduced *Send in the Clowns* on Broadway. In one of the episodes, I got to play and flirt with huge triple threat star Van Johnson. What a pleasure. With our super cast, *Coming of Age* should've been as big a hit as *Golden Girls.* It was about seniors in a retirement community. Who can laugh about themselves and sex more than seniors? In my humble opinion, CBS censored good material to the point of boredom.

Jake and the Fatman (William Conrad) - TV This was a double treat, a great role to play that took me to location in Hawaii. Webb joined me there and it was wonderful to spend time with *Hollywood Squares,* Mary and Gary Damsker, my longest-term friends, who were living there.

This was the first time that I worked with Bill Conrad, a great motion picture and television actor and radio veteran. The Fatman and I loved visiting between takes. (Side Note) Many of the *Gunsmoke* television episodes starring Jim Arness were video versions of the original radio broadcasts starring Bill himself.

He was unfortunately riddled with diabetes. His feet were in very, very bad shape. He was carrying around all that extra weight. It broke my heart because he would not stop indulging in the *tasty* things in life. He was the first actor I knew that didn't need me or any of his co-stars to read the lines to him on his close-ups. Bill brought his characters to life on radio and clearly that applied to television as well. He gave me his recording of *The 12 Days of Christmas* that is so outrageously funny, that I don't wait for Christmas to play it.

Charles in Charge - TV: Scott Baio of *Happy Days and Joanie Loves Chachi* was so cute to work with. I tried to get him to be the new young person to take over for *The Thalians.* NO LUCK! This show introduced me to a whole new generation of fans, as did my stint on *Power Rangers* and so the younger beat goes on.

Murder She Wrote - TV: Working with iconic Angela Lansbury, is always a pleasure. I've tried to emulate her. She can do it all. Angela introduced Mame to the world, a part that I have loved and played all over the country, unfortunately, never on Broadway.

Angela ages gracefully and continues working on Broadway and film, also giving time to meet charitable requests. With much persuasion, she agreed to be *The Thalians* honoree in our All-Star show. Debbie and I were delighted to receive kudos from Jerry Herman for our performance of *Bosom Buddies* (from Mame), a great compliment. The same applies to our buddy, Ron Masak (the sheriff), who lends his talent, personality and golfing skills to many charitable endeavors.

Ruta-Angela-Debbie ...I'm in the
company and friendship of 2
Superstars

Bonnie Hunt - TV: Bonnie is one of my favorite ladies. She does the best imitation of Ruta Lee. I have guested on several of her shows, but the silly blonde bitch didn't have me on her last talk show. Obviously, that's why it was cancelled [wink, wink].

Funny Bones-Jerry Lewis-Leslie Caron on location in Blackpool UK

Funny Bones - Movie: Jerry Lewis, Leslie Caron, Lee Evans, Oliver Platt and Oliver Reed. This movie shot mostly in England, now a cult favorite, should and could have been a huge hit for Disney Studios. At the time, there was a big change of regime there. The incoming chairman didn't care to support what the outgoing had considered his favorite. So, in spite of four-star reviews in previews, marketing monies went to promote Pocahontas, which went up in smoke ... signals.

After many years of friendship, I was finally working with Jerry Lewis. He had always loved the ladies and was surrounded by them. If Jerry ever made a pass at me, I didn't recognize it. Maybe that's why we're friends. When I was working at Paramount, I'd sometimes visit on his set. He always had the most current electronic toys available. I commented on his nifty phonograph (or record player for you kids) that played all three speeds of vinyl. The next thing I knew, one had been delivered to my house. I've used it for years.

Jerry, proud father of 7 boys was now married to a beautiful lady named Sam, who thrilled him by giving birth to a beautiful baby girl. He was a very happy camper.

During filming in England and Vegas, I spent all of my spare time with Jerry, talking in the dressing room, walking on the beach, whatever. It was satisfying to relive so much history, not so much together, but around both of us that brought us together. One night we were at Simpsons, the Prime Rib place to be in London. The décor is quite English with high backed booths. That night, the restaurant was filled with Japanese tourists. While telling a story, he stood up delivering a punch line and all the Japanese gasped, pointed and said "Rook, Jelly Rewis and Luta Ree!" We slid under the table with laughter and delight. When the team of Martin and Lewis split, it was said, "Dean Martin will die on the vine." Well, as we all know, Dean became a huge star. Jerry remained continually successful. He was idolized by the French, who awarded him the Legion of Honor, loved by the Brits and clearly loved by the Japanese. He survived in his personal life better than Dean, who understandably, fell apart after the tragic death of his son. Jerry was more fortunate. He was happy with his family, his many awards and philanthropy, which has helped so many in this world.

Pterodactyl Woman of Beverly Hills - Movie: with Beverly D'Angelo and I don't know who else ... except Barbara Stuart and myself. Oops, I forgot Barry Humphries a.k.a. the fabulous Dame Edna. I've never seen this movie and wonder if I ever will.

Quiet Kill - Movie: Corbin Bernsen, damn good actor and why not? His mom, soap operas Jeanne Cooper was the leading lady icon of Y&R. In her youth, she was also the leading lady in a production of On the Town at the Gallery Stage, in which I was a chorus girl. I was still in high school and just beginning my career when I was noticed by an associate producer of the Burns and Allen how. That landed me my first television job and my SAG Card.

Sadie and the Slot Machines - Movie: A film done by AFI students. It's a nice piece of work, a lovely little, short movie. My leading man was Steve Rossi with whom I had a three-year run of Senior Class in Palm Springs. The team of Marty Allen and Steve Rossi guested on the Ed Sullivan Show more than anyone else.

Christmas Do Over - Jay Mohr was in this. He's so cute and made me laugh the entire time, a really good stand-up comic. What I love most about him is that he let me talk him in to performing for *The Thalians*. Adrienne Barbeau, Daphne Zuniga and David Millbern were great to work with. Daphne came to *The Thalians* and bought the hybrid car we had for auction. She's a rare one of the new generation. She gives back.

A Christmas Too Many - Movie: I worked with the legendary Mickey Rooney and Marla Maples on this film. Mickey and I knew each other well, socially, but he had forgotten that I had worked with him 50 years earlier on *The Twinkle in God's Eye.*

By the way, Marla Maples is one of Donald Trump's ex's and we dished a little on "The Donald." The night before my 6 am call, I was bitten by a weird bug, a cone nosed beetle, went into anaphylactic shock and wound up being taken by ambulance to the hospital. They gave me a big dose of antihistamine and insisted I stay the night. I said, "Bullshit, I start a movie in the morning." Needless to say, I got to the set on time and filmed.

Christmas at Cadillac Jacks - Movie: The leading man is longtime friend, Joe Campanella and lovely actress Talia Shire (of Rocky fame) plays my daughter. This is one of the movies that is aired every Christmas season and was beautifully cast by my special friend Chauncey Smith.

For Better or For Worse - Movie: David Arquette was sweet. Bijou Phillips, was loopy, don't know what she was on. This new wave film production is strange. In my opinion we have lost the professionalism and discipline required. We seem to find bizarre behavior acceptable.

Sweet Bird of Youth - TV Movie - Elizabeth Taylor- Mark Harmon - I played a Hedda Hopper type columnist. What

I remember most about the shoot was a lot of waiting around for Liz. What made the waiting more tolerable was chatting with her son Michael Wilding Jr. who was playing his father of same name. He was charming as was his dad. Nolan Miller designed the wardrobe for Liz, so she and I had that in common... besides Debbie, that is.

Throughout much of my career, I was a leading lady. Playing roles is like a dance. I could only be as good as my partner and vice versa. Together, we played off each other. My life and career has been filled with the support of memorable men and women. I'm thankful to all of them for the memories and a career that has lasted six decades.

Most of the people I'm talking about remained my friends. We laughed our way through everything. Affairs were never an issue, because it was all too laughable. I was the lady that the guys could go have a beer with. We always sat around, told bawdy stories using dirty language. We enjoyed that in lieu of fun between the sheets.

Chapter 13

The Leading Man in My Life

If I'd gotten married when I was very young, who knows, I might have had children of my own. Instead, I'm blessed with stepchildren, Godchildren, a great extended family ... and best of all no stretch marks. As a young woman, I was always independent. I wasn't hungry, lived well, had great cars, clothes and dated every man in this world at least once... some interesting and cultured, some not.

I thought about marriage at different times ... but, there wasn't anybody I cared to spend the rest of my life with and then, well into my thirties, I met Webb Lowe.

I was in a highly successful run of *Goodbye Charlie* in a Dallas theater. The six-week run was coming to a close, when the producers came to me and said, "Our next show isn't selling well. Would you play an extra week, which would give us time to promote the upcoming show?"

I said, "I can't. We are supposed to close Sunday night and Monday morning I'm expected in Naples, Florida by the LPGA to be the guest star at their opening ceremonies." These golfers were giving me an honorarium of $10,000 for my Thalians, which in 1974, was a hell of a lot of money.

My producers suggested, "Take Monday off. Come back in time to do a show on Tuesday and give us an extra show on the weekend." Ok! Done deal. I'd had the flu for weeks, wasn't feeling great, could use the day off to rest, but thought, 'What the hell?', I had committed. So I got on the plane and flew to Miami. It was February and I was wearing a fur coat. It was hot in Miami. A little private plane picked me up and flew me over to Naples.

I fluffed up for this personal appearance. I pulled out the feather boa. I put on a pretty dress, stuck on eyelashes, in preparation for a parade with the mayor, followed by the banquet with the Ladies Professional Golf Association. All went very well in spite of exacerbating my cold.

The next day I felt awful, tired, hot, feverish and I had to take the little plane back to Miami and then American Airlines back to Dallas for the show that night. There I was, at the check-in counter, my hair pulled back under a babushka, not a stitch of makeup, wearing big dark glasses, dabbing my red runny nose. They took pity on me and said, "Happy Valentines Ms. Lee. We'll pre-board you as soon as the plane is ready."

I sniffled my "Thanks." and stood there wilting. Knowing I had a show to do that night, all I wanted to do was get on the plane and sleep for two hours. I was leaning head down on the counter, looked down the hall and saw a great pair of Gucci loafers coming toward me. I looked up a little further and saw nice slacks, with a crease in them and a double-breasted blazer with gold buttons. Looking up further, there's that face, a shock of silver hair... a cross between Clint Eastwood and Peter Graves. I thought ... 'Hello handsome!' Those shoes walked toward my check-in counter... toward and toward and right past me, down the corridor. I thought, 'Oh shit, ships that pass in the night.'

They pre-boarded me. I plopped my fur on the seat next to me, asked for a glass of water and took a Dristan. I pulled down the pillow and blanket; I was going to sleep. As I was stowing my carry on under the seat, I looked down and the same Gucci's were standing there. He looked down at my coat and asked, "Is this seat taken?" I replied, "for the last time in my life no!" He said, "Hello, my name is Webb Lowe!!!"

I said, "Hello my name is Ruta Lee and we should be married, because then I'd be Ruta Lee Lowe and we could open a Chinese laundry." He laughed and we talked and talked. I forgot I was sick. He didn't know what a Ruta Lee was. He didn't know any movie people beyond John Wayne. We talked about California wines and how underrated they were. Wine was a big topic. I invited him to see my show in Dallas before it closed that week.

I also told him that my next job was going to be in San Diego, playing *Irma la Douce*. "Drop in, if you're going to be in that neighborhood." He said that he travelled a great deal and might be able to make that happen. We exchanged cards.

When I arrived at the theater that evening, I found a huge batch of yellow roses. The card said, "Happy Valentine's Day. Sorry, I won't be able to make this one. I'll catch the next one twice." I thought, 'Oh be still my disappointed heart.' I told my cast mates, "These are from a man I should marry. He's a real find."

A few weeks later, I was in San Diego and in rehearsals for *Irma*. It was hard work and great fun. John McCook (of Bold and the Beautiful) was my leading man in the play and Juliet Prowse's leading man in life. Irma was a signature role for Juliet. On opening night, you can imagine how nervous I was with her in the front row, me playing *her* role with *her* husband.

On my day off I came home to LA to find a beautiful coffee table book on California wine. Webb's card said, "We talked of these wines and I thought you'd enjoy this." I called his office. He was President/CEO of Bonanza, a nationwide chain of steakhouses with offices based in Dallas. His secretary said, "He's in a meeting. I'll tell him you called."

Five minutes later he called back. "I think I'm going to be in San Diego soon. I'll find you." I came into the theater one night to find my tiny dressing room, overflowing with flowers. His note said, "I couldn't get a ticket last night, but I'm here tonight and have a good show."

Of course I spotted him in the third row, the minute I made my entrance and played the entire show to him.

You have to remember the cast was eighteen guys and me.

After the show, I sent out for a bottle of champagne and had it brought to the dressing room. I was thinking, 'I'm finally going to spend a little time with this Mr. Wonderful.' Of course, he, not knowing shit from shinola about protocol in theater, never came backstage. I had the ushers looking under the seats to see if he'd passed out or something, because he never came back. I thought, 'He hated the show. He didn't want to say anything.' Weeks passed until we talked on the phone. He explained. "It was you and all those fellas. I figured you'd be very busy. I didn't want to interrupt. I didn't want to overstep."

Many phone conversations ensued, however, our next meeting was in Austin, where I was again doing *Goodbye Charlie*. He was there for a conference at Lakeway, a resort outside of Austin. He came to see the show. We went out for a late supper. Clearly the attraction between us was growing. The hour was late so I invited him to use my guest room, rather than take the long drive back to Lakeway, some 30 miles from Austin. He responded, "No, I have a meeting in the morning. It's best that I go back tonight."

Then he called me in the morning saying, "Why don't you come out and have lunch with me at Lakeway?" I did. He was not in business clothes. He was in a pair of jeans and barefoot in soft loafers. I looked at that man and my heart skipped several beats.

That afternoon , I drove him to the airport, waved goodbye, wondering what our future might hold.

Between theater engagements, my life in LA continued at its hectic pace, which included dating several men. One afternoon Webb called from San Francisco. He was heading to Dallas but could swing through LA if I was available for dinner. I had a prior dinner date, which I told Webb I could cancel, reschedule, or the three of us could go. I CANCELLED!

Webb arrived at my house, a veritable Prince Charming, carrying a colorful Papier-Mache pony and cart filled with straw flowers, which I still have. In typical motherly fashion, mine peeked through the curtains and commented, "God should only bless you with this kind of man." For once, I agreed.

That evening became pivotal, because Webb had a pressing need and desire to explain the status of his failed marriage ... his life, his work, his family and how it would affect us. He shared that the divorce papers had been filed long before we met. However, everything was on hold temporarily.

Why? He was considerate and respectful of his mother- in-law, who was in the last stages of cancer. They were truly fond of each other.

He and his wife Kitty had agreed not to cause her more pain at the close of her life. I admired his compassion and appreciated his honesty and his wish not to involve me in a situation, which to some could appear tawdry. While we obviously had feelings for each other, we had to this point, not acted upon them, nor would we. Time, prayer and patience brought closure to these unresolved issues, allowing us the freedom to explore a future together.

Several months later, he came to see me in St Louis, where I was once again playing *Charlie* with the same cast. By now, they knew I was more than a little smitten and had more than a crush on this guy. So I said, "Ok, it's our night off. Let's all meet up for, "Welcome Webb drinks," but then I want everybody to get lost and leave us alone. He arrived at the building that the cast resided in, looking like the man from Glad. He was in a white suit with a beautiful windowpane blue shirt, gorgeous tie... and of course the white hair. He's a handsome man, but when he's put together, he's divine! There he was, carrying a great big package of vodka in an iced bucket. He had caviar to go with the vodka. That was a bit of ok, which we all enjoyed and then per direction the "cast" made an exit.

After a quiet, romantic dinner, I once again invited Webb to use my guest room and this time he did! However, there was little time for romance. That was the night I was calling Lucille Ball in Hollywood to be our Thalians honoree. With the three-hour time difference calls went back and forth the whole evening, with Lucy finally saying "YES." Webb and I both were exhausted. I retired to my room and he to the guest room ... well part of the night. Lucy wasn't the only one who said yes that night.

Our relationship was here to stay and we continued this long-distance courtship all across the country, wherever our schedules took us. Often, we spent time at his townhouse in Dallas. It wasn't a whirlwind courtship. We got to know each other well. We determined we were meant for each other and in preparation for our marriage, bought a house in Greenway Park, Dallas. On Valentine's Day Eve 1976 ...Friday the 13th... in a bicentennial and leap year, we were married. The owners of the Beverly Hills Hotel, Muriel and Burt Slatkin graciously hosted our wedding at their home with the reception held at the hotel for an intimate group of seventy-five. World famous designer, Nolan Miller of *Dynasty* fame, created my wedding gown.

The next night, St. Valentines, Hugh Hefner, hosted a reception for four hundred dazzling stars and celebrities at the Playboy Mansion. It was an incredible affair with thirty violinists flanking the entry hall and hanging floral baskets holding live doves, everywhere. The paparazzi had a field day. I wore a gown by Travilla (who created the famous Marilyn Monroe subway dress that Debbie Reynolds sold at auction for 5 million dollars). Webb and I greeted each guest, got pulled aside to cut the cake and take pictures, with host Hugh and his then lady Barbie Benton. Before we knew it, we were saying good night to each and every guest. We never had one bite of the sumptuous, white glove service dinner. We got home that night and had peanut butter and jelly sandwiches.

Mr. and Mrs. Webb Lowe Wedding
Reception – Playboy Mansion with Hef and
Barbie Benton

I often think about the fact that Webb and I have clicked for a lifetime. When his first marriage failed, it was not because he was looking outside his marriage for a tootsie. It was over long before I entered the picture. They simply grew in different directions.

They had four children, grown teenagers by then. He tried very hard to secure their education and future. After we were married, we moved into our honeymoon house in Greenway Park. One evening, Webb was on the phone, with Kitty, his ex. He said, "If you're going to drop the girls off, then come on in and have a drink with us." I then heard, "Well ok, see you in a few minutes." Oh, I looked like shit, and this would be the first time I meet the ex. I ran upstairs and fluffed up the hair and put on a pretty little hostess gown. Now I heard them at the front door, which was at the bottom of our lovely staircase. I did a Loretta Young showgirl walk all the way down. I almost hummed the music.

Kitty and her beau were there watching my grand entrance. We looked at each other. We both opened our arms and hugged. She said, "Thank you for being so good to my children. Thank you, you're a doll." We both burst into tears, a wet start of a unique and loving friendship with my "wife in-law" which lasted many years until her untimely death from lung cancer. She smoked to the end.

As a stepmother, to four young people, I did the best I could for them, even though our interests were different. They were never an imposition. I enjoyed doing events for and around them. The now adult kids have provided many grandchildren, who are so special. But please note, they're Webb's grandchildren. I refuse to be called grandma. They call me Ruta.

Of the four children, the eldest, Webb III (Sonny) was a bad boy type. He was smart as a whip, but if there was trouble, he'd find it and he was always in it. In his teens he had gotten into drugs. We thought the marines would straighten him out, so we encouraged him to join. While stationed overseas he married a darling girl. Sadly, after return, they divorced. He soon married another. While he was married to Juanita and she was having one of his babies, a mistress that he also had, was having his other baby at the same time in the same hospital.

Sonny became ill. Perhaps it was the drugs. Perhaps it was lifestyle. Perhaps bad medical attention. He died too young. He lived in McAllen, very South Texas. Having been a Marine, he had lots of Marine buddies there, all of whom hung out at some honky-tonk saloon. When he died, Webb and I went to South Texas to join the wonderful Juanita, Kitty, her husband and Sonny's siblings for the memorial. He loved fishing, so his friend, a fishing boat captain, graciously volunteered to take us out to scatter his ashes at sea.

We went to the funeral home to pick up his cremated remains. I don't know if you've dealt with anything like this but much to my surprise, when I got to the hotel, I discovered the ashes were not what I expected. I had purchased little silver and shelled boxes so that each family member could keep some ashes as a remembrance. I opened the box of ashes assuming that a piece of paper could scoop out the ashes for distribution. No such thing! It's like a block of porous cement, hard as a rock. There was some loose ash, but very little. I went down to the hotel kitchen and borrowed a big carving knife and spoon. I then sat and started chipping away at this block. I divvied it up the best I could. This is bizarre, should be a funny scene in a movie.

The family took the long drive to the boat. Finally, we got out on the water. Oops, nobody thought to bring a minister or cleric. Naturally, I took the lead and started to say some nice things about Sonny. Everybody said a little something. In short order the captain stopped the boat. We scattered the ashes...kerplunk, scattered flowers, held hands, said the Lord's Prayer and saluted Sonny with a much-needed glass or three of wine. We headed back to McAllen where Sonny's military buddies determined that the back yard of his favorite saloon was an appropriate setting for his memorial. They planned a twenty-one-gun salute. Traffic and distance caused us to be about an hour late. Hell, by the time we arrived, they were all sloshed. They didn't know what they were doing. They had their guns out and all I could think, was 'Holy mackerel, we're going to get shot by his firing squad.'

Taps was played, not by a heart-rending solitary bugler, but on a rinky-dink tape recorder. For Webb, this was all too surreal. I just saw the whole thing like a scene in a strange movie. The salute started, first they fired off a few rounds and one of the riflemen said and I quote, "BANG! BANG! Well shiiiiiit, mine's not firin!" They didn't quite get to shot twenty-one, maybe seven...which was more than enough for me. That was his big send-off. We didn't know whether to laugh or cry, so we did both.

Thank God Webb and I have managed to laugh our way through 46 years of the "better and worse" He is my placid port when times are stormy and I must tell you, I bubble in contentment when people comment on how he looks at me … with such love. Webb claims that I am the sails, he is the rudder on our ship of life. I'm blessed to have Webb as my leading man forever. I know he feels the same about his leading lady, in spite of the fact that after all these years, still no Lee-Lowe Laundry as promised.

Oh, a happy memory - Phyllis Diller's Birthday was July 17th. Webb's is July 18th and Alex's is July 22nd...which always gave us good reason to celebrate the three with one star filled celebration.

I am so incredibly grateful for the many blessed and happy years we shared. Just before Christmas 2017 Webb suffered a stroke which did not paralyze his body, however it did affect his brain. This was the onset of dementia which needless to say effected both our lives daily. When God doled out my blessings, He was most generous in many ways, but he shorted me on patience. Oh boy I am learning every day how important that virtue is. I am keeping Webb at home with me. With the help of his caregiver Loel De Los Santos and Major Domo my cousin Ona Katilius, we are managing extremely well. I am sure the time will come when for his well- being and security a nursing home will become a reality rather than an option. Thank God Webb has always been a mild-mannered gentle man. With the help of my dearest friend Dr. Lawrence Piro who oversees his condition and meds Webb is able to be and do well in his own home. Dr. Piro, world renowned oncologist, is the head honcho at his outstanding all-encompassing

Angeles Clinic and Research Institute in Santa Monica. I know many of you are having similar experiences. I pray that we all use our reserves of love to help our loved one and ourselves survive and thrive.

As we are about to go to print, this beautiful chapter on the love of my life, now has a very painful closing. My handsome Webb went to meet his loving God and his best pals that preceded him through the pearly gates. I grieve for my love but take great comfort in reflecting on our precious 46 years together.

He was the perfect husband, and I can honestly say we never had cross words between us. I learned an important lesson from Webb that I'd like to share with new brides. That first year of togetherness, I like most girls, was super sensitive. He didn't answer me quickly- he didn't remember flowers - he snapped at me - I responded to all with pouting and tears. Webb said... "Ruta, tomorrow will this be important ? at the end of the week-month- year?" We laughed then and in future over all disagreements.

I am grateful for the thousands of condolence messages, flowers and contributions to *The Thalians* in memory of my Webb. The universal theme is that he was the ultimate gentleman. Amen and thank you Webb, you made my life beautiful...I will always love you.

One of the 46 anniversaries we celebrated

Chapter 14

Deep in the Heart of Texas

My beloved friend and sister in charity, Debbie Reynolds had the good fortune to be born in Texas. I wasn't, but there are lots of people there who would challenge you to a fistfight if you say that. However, I have claimed this great state and have become an official resident in Fort Worth. If it hadn't been for Texas, I wouldn't have met Webb, or many of the people that I've called family and friends for so many years.

Ruta as Mollie Brown at her favorite theater Casa Mañana

To this day, Fort Worth and it's Casa Mañana Theater are my favorites in the country and the name Ruta Lee and Casa Mañana are synonymous. It all started in 1964, when the theater's director Michael Pollock came to meet me in New York, as I was returning from my much-publicized Lithuanian adventure. He was savvy enough to realize that any spunky little girl, tough enough to go up against the Soviet bureaucrats, would be an ideal lead for his production of the *Unsinkable Molly Brown* in the upcoming summer line up. The money wasn't great, but he talked me into it, saying, "Ruta, you won't regret it." Oh, how right he was!

Along with Michael, I owe a debt of gratitude to the Fort Worth press icons, whom I met my first day in the city. A "howdy-meet-the-star" breakfast had been arranged with the press at the Petroleum Club, which turned out to be a hilarious love fest. Elston Brooks, Bobbie Wygant, Jack Gordon, Tony Slaughter, Perry Stewart are just some of the people who put me on the front pages, introducing me to a wonderful, hospitable city. Well, I fell in love with Fort Worth and thankfully the feeling was mutual. Bobbie Wygant, NBC's voice and Texas personality for three quarters of a century is still as pretty and active as the day we met.

The "Unsinkable Molly Brown" was a roaring success with unparalleled reviews, among which was the published statement from the "Music Man" himself, Meredith Willson (Molly Brown's writer/composer), who was in the opening night audience: "Ruta is the best Molly of them all. If she had been playing it on

Broadway, it would still be running." That endorsement was like icing on my very bruised body. Those routines were rigorous, but so worth it. That was also the night when making a rapid exit through swinging doors, I tripped over a door sill (that hadn't been there during rehearsal) and literally flew over the orchestra pit into the first row. Thank God, my dear girlfriend Peggy King, who had just closed in "Mr. President", stood up, reached out and we both hit the floor. Peggy got bruises as well...one more of the many fun experiences we've shared through a lifetime.

Another one of my many bruising moments was during *Woman of the Year,* some years later, when a big burley dancer did a big burley turn on my poor little foot. Two broken toes, lots of ice, screaming in pain, replacing my shoe, but ... amazing how you forget pain when that orchestra is playing and you're on!!!

Every season, Casa house Doctor, Ed Etier, came to treat my wounds and give me B-12 shots. (Ed had been a chorus boy in the original Billy Rose Casa Mañana.) When I pulled down my bloomers to get the shot, he went into shock at the black and blue marks from knees to buns. No, no, I was not a masochist, those were bruises proudly earned by being lifted and tossed in all the numbers. Ed took me into his heart and his family.

The 2,000-seat theater was filled every night during my runs and prompted producers Mel Dacus and later, Bud Franks to invite me back the next year and the next and the next ... for some forty years. I got to play just about every part that I ever wanted. The audiences embraced each character that I brought to life for them. One of those characters almost didn't come to life, "Irene".

Debbie Reynolds, the ultimate "Unsinkable" onscreen and off, didn't let me sink when I was in my Casa dressing room, drowning in the depths of despair. Lousy costumes had arrived from Brooks Costumes New York, just two days before the opening of *Irene. M*y brilliant cast member friend, Bruce Lee and his wife, Frances, had worked with Debbie in *Irene* on Broadway. He called her and she saved the day and the show, by sending out all her personal Irene costumes just in the nick of time. A great example of her Texas generosity!

Let me digress a moment with a piece of Casa Mañana history. The original outdoor theater was built by Fort Worth billionaire, Amon Carter, because he wouldn't spend a single dime at the Dallas outdoor theater entertainment center ... CITY RIVALRIES! He contracted the infamous Billy Rose, then married to the famous Fanny Brice and they built an entertainment palace with a tall spectacular water fountain for a main curtain, that masked the innovative revolving stage. The water lowered for the performances and raised again to close them.

This was decades before Dancing Waters! Adjoining was a full carnival midway, featuring the notorious SALLY RAND'S NUDE RANCH! I met her many years later, got to know and love her. Sally had a salty tongue and told me many stories of her friendship with Fanny Brice. She said

Fanny's husband, the gifted, but womanizing Billy Rose was a #1 shit.

Years later, now well into her 80's Sally was still performing her scandalous, feather fan dance. She was appearing in a Fort Worth club and I invited the cast of my Casa show to see her late, late show. Earlier that evening, she had asked me to put eyelashes on her, claiming, "I'm an old broad I can't see."

Shot for Esquire Magazine – Maybe I could have
appeared at Sally Rand's Nude Ranch

I wondered how in hell at her age, she'd pull off nude dancing. Well, she did ... with panache! Amazing, what a blue light, a body stocking, glitter on strategic places and sultry music can do. We all became her fans and cheerleaders. Over time, the original Casa Theater went into disrepair. In the mid 50's world famous Buckminster Fuller was called upon to design the geodesic dome that became the renowned Casa Mañana we know today.

Casa, like all live theaters, has financial struggles and created many fundraising activities. At one of these events, I was an auction item. The offer was dinner with Ruta Lee and twelve guests at Eddie V's., a renowned Fort Worth eatery. Casa patrons, whom I'd never met, Judi and Gary Martin, made a really generous bid and won the prize, me!

At the appointed time, Webb and I walked into the restaurant, shook hands, kissed hello and went into nonstop conversation as if we had been friends for fifty years. My new best friend, Gary Martin is very philanthropic and has become a great supporter of *The Thalians*, flying his planeload of friends out for our events. Again, Texas generosity at its best.

The love I've always felt from Texas audiences is overwhelming. They do not defy you to entertain them. They come into the theater to have a good time, jump on the bandwagon and enjoy the ride. Yahoo y'all!

Sugar Babies – Hats off to all my audiences

What a joyous ride we have shared. A few years back, I returned to Casa in *Hello Dolly*. Opening night, as I made my second act entrance down the famous Harmonia Garden stairs, singing that familiar theme song: "Hello

Harry. Well, hello Louie. It's so great to be back home where I belong." The entire audience stood and started applauding like crazy, while conductor; Joe Stecko just stood there, shrugged and laid down the baton. It was hard to continue.

My throat choked up and tears welled up. We just waited until it all calmed down. It was overwhelming to get that kind of love thrown at you.

Ruta – Carol Channing – Debbie....
2 Dolly's and a Molly

Oh sure, I received the expected and appreciated applause on my first entrance, but this took my breath away, to hear the audience agreeing with lyrics, "Nice have you back where you belong." Show stopping, heart stopping ... my pinnacle moment in theater.

A lot of my Hollywood friends shared that moment, as my girlfriend, Paula Kent Meehan had brought them in on her private jet. It was an amazing evening that none of us will ever forget.

I'll also never forget the last time I did The Best Little Whore House ... the gal from the box office said, "There's a mother, daughter and granddaughter that have flown in from Ruidoso, New Mexico to see the matinee. They would like to see you after the show. Her name is Ruta Lee. "Great! Have them come on back. Anybody that traveled all the way from Ruidoso and is named Ruta Lee should come backstage." They did and I said, "You really just flew in to see my show?"

The daughter said, "Mom here, is a big fan of yours. She always loved you. When I was born, she named me Ruta Lee, so we came to see my namesake and idol. That's all I ever wanted." I said, "Well, are you going to stay for a while? Are you visiting other people, while you're here?" "No, we're flying back in the morning." "Well, why don't you go have dinner, come back this evening and see the show again, as my guests." So they did.

After final bows in every show, I step out of character and "Ruta" chats with the audience. We share some personal moments some humor and I express my gratitude for their presence. This particular evening, I introduced the Ruidoso Ruta, her mother and daughter to the audience, telling their story, garnering sweet applause. My namesake will cherish that experience forever... so will I.

A Texan I idolized was Mary Martin, a Broadway Legend. She was exceedingly talented and lucky to play major shows that went down in history...South Pacific, Sound of Music, Peter Pan, I Do I Do. Famous, Neiman Marcus, hair stylist, Jay Wallace, was my Casa hair stylist. I always claimed him as my BIG brother (and he was at 6 x 6). He also styled Mary's sister, Geraldine's hair and saw to it that we met. Gerri referred to Mary as Sissy and she'd tell me, "Dahlin, ya'll so much like mah Sissy, I can't tell you. I can't tell you child. You walk, talk and do all the same things that she does." My voice was deeper, but that's about it. Fortunately, I got to play some of the roles that Mary made famous and made her a legend.

The Thalians selected and were delighted to have Mary Martin as an honoree and she became my good friend. At that Thalians show, I did "Honeybun", Mary's number from South Pacific with the wonderful Ray Walston. Needless to say, it was terrifying doing her famous number before the Broadway queen herself.

Mary said, "I got so sick of hearing about you from my sister Gerri in Texas. Ruta, she's right. You are as wonderful as my Gerri says you are." That was heaven sent, to have my idol become my friend. The same can be said of my friendships with Mitzi Gaynor, June Haver, Ethel Merman, Betty Grable, Lana Turner, Jane Wyman and wonderful Carol Channing.

Mary, one of our most beloved honorees, returned the following year to perform with Lucille Ball, Shirley Jones, Sammy Davis in the All-star tribute to Music Man Robert Preston.

My idol – Mary Martin

Mary "Sissy" Martin was not the only Sissy in my life. Casa's stage manager, Florine, known as Sissy Pully, has been a helping hand and loving influence. This marvelous person took amazing care of all company members in her capable hands. After several years of working together, I knew she could direct with the best of them and asked the producers to have her direct my "Annie Get Your Gun." I'm proud to say it was a beautiful production, one of Casa's best. Thank you Sissy. She went on to direct many, many shows in Houston, before retiring to Ft. Worth. She is now directing for the master producer in heaven.

Casa also gave me a dear friend, Judy Mc Elhannon. She came to almost every performance of mine at Casa Mañana, I said, "You know, you're being in the audience every show is crazy. Why don't you come to work for the theater, at least when I'm working here?" She did and had the responsibility of running me up and down the aisles, helping me with my lines, or whatever was needed. She was a great right hand. Judy kept so much press and marketing material on me, she could've opened the Ruta Lee Museum. Unfortunately, she had a fire at her home and a great deal of that material was lost. Thank God, not all. Our friendship, however, will never be lost.

Guardian Angel/Godson Scott Deshong

Jay Wallace brought in a big coterie of Texans each year to *The Thalians* Ball. He made that and a lot of things possible. However, he did the impossible with my hair in the most impossible places.

There was washing my hair on a sink counter in a restaurant during a television shoot, airplane galleys, combing me out in filling station rest rooms. The topper was Carlsbad Caverns for a news story... hairspray and bat guano.

If not for Jay, I would not have known Mary Martin and Sally Rand. Whether it was celebrities, fans, friends or family, he kept adding Texans to my life. Jay Wallace also introduced me to my now Godson, Scott DeShong. He said to Scotty, "You need Ruta and she will need you." He was so right. Scott and his partner Brian Theobald are essential to my life in every way. They are my beloved chosen family.

Jay, as his health was fading (diabetes) brought a young apprentice, hairdresser (now Fort Worth/ Hollywood hair stylist) David Blackstock into my dressing room to help with my hair. David stayed and continues to help in my life. He and his husband Tony Colbert are now considered family. My boys/men are the sons I didn't have to birth. As I said before, no stretch marks!

David continues to do my hair in Fort Worth and in Hollywood. I happily shared him with celebrities that visited Texas, like Joan Rivers, Debbie Reynolds, Sally Struthers and the wonderful Ruth Buzzi. Ruth joined her gorgeous Texan, husband, Kent Perkins and become residents of Fort Worth. Ruth, of course, is now a permanent client/friend of David's. We spend many hours together at every opportunity. I'm always welcome at their beautiful plantation/Sunset Ranch...their bit of Texas heaven.

David Blackstock and Tony Colbert – my
Texas family

There are so many more colorful people, places and
events in Texas that have filled my life and heart. For
instance, Houston was an out of this world experience.
Not only did I have an enjoyable run with Judd Hirsch
there at the Country Dinner Playhouse, but that's where
I formed lasting friendships with many of our American
hero astronauts. Johnson Space Center was home and
work to a lot of the original astronauts. It was truly
thrilling to be guided through the center exhibits by
these heroes.

After being inside one of the modules, I realized that claustrophobia would have prevented me from even considering space flight.

When business brought any of them to Los Angeles, Shirley MacLaine and I were their unofficial Hollywood hostesses. One or the other would take the responsibility of hosting dinner for these marvelous men. To be honest, it was big thrill for both of us to show off these heroes to our Hollywood friends. It was also a thrill to introduce many of them to audiences when they came to see one of my shows. Hell, they always got a standing ovation.

Walt Cunningham and his wife remained very good friends. I'm happy that my darling Pete Conrad was a great Space Center host on a segment of my interview show, *Talk of the Town.*

Pete and his wife, Nancy, had agreed to chair *The Thalians* Ball for me just before Pete was killed in motorcycle mishap. Friends, can you imagine, three trips to the moon and it was a crash on a country road in Ojai, CA. that ended his life? Nancy Conrad bravely continued the Ball preparations and fourteen of the original astronauts honored Pete's memory and *The Thalians* at the 44th Annual Ball.

As each mission was announced, that flight's astronaut stepped into an astral light. All fourteen originals, Nancy stepping in for Pete, filled the stage for the first and only time. What awesome history and memories we made!

... a poignant and fitting farewell to space hero Pete Conrad, one that all in attendance will never ever forget.

These American heroes, who flew amongst the stars, far outshone our Hollywood stars that evening. You can see why I'm grateful to Texas. I got a perfect husband, best friends, a sister Debbie Reynolds, adventures with astronauts, 40 years of extraordinary theatrical experiences and the ongoing love affair with the greatest little city in the world, Fort Worth.

The Original Early Astronauts left to right: Thomas Mattingly, Bill Anders, Buzz Aldrin, Charles Walker, Walter Cunningham, Richard Gordon, Mae Jemison, Russell Schweickart, Bob Peterson - front row: Debbie Reynolds, Gerald Griffin, Gordon Cooper, Margie Peterson, Kathy Sullivan, Nancy Conrad, Alan Bean, Ruta Lee

Chapter 15

Not So Dumb Blondes

Marilyn Monroe has been universally acknowledged as the première "glow girl" and indeed she was. I met her only once. Frank Sinatra was throwing a birthday party for Dean Martin at the Sands, Las Vegas, where Dean was headlining. It was a celebrity filled showroom and I was surrounded by the biggest names in show business. At Frank's table seated on either side of me were Milton Berle and John Wayne. (Be still my heart.) Across the table was Elizabeth Taylor, then married to Eddie Fisher. Elizabeth was stunning at the height of her beauty. However, when Marilyn walked in with Frank, the room gasped. She shimmered in sequins and white fox.... breathtakingly beautiful. She seemed to have an inner spotlight that stole the focus from the beautiful Liz and kept it all evening.

The masters of taking focus and lighting a room with their presence were the Gabors... not just the girls, Zsa Zsa, Eva and Magda, but Mama Jolie herself. I met Jolie at the Palm Springs Playhouse when I was the ingénue in a play staring, Victor Jory. She had come to see the play with a coterie of friends and I was fortunate enough to be included in their after-show supper plans. Jolie in that unmistakable Gabor accent said, "Rutahh dahhling, you look like my daughters. I adopt you." Wow! What a compliment!

She was then married to Edmund, some 30 years her junior. I dared to ask her how that came to be. She replied, "Oh dahhling, I love him from the day Zsa Zsa brought him home from school."

Jolie had a wonderful costume jewelry store on Madison Avenue in NYC, which I frequented every time I got there. Magda had a fabulous townhouse on 5th Avenue to which I was invited on several occasions. It was thrilling to be in the company of New York's most beautiful social set. Thank you Jolie!

Jolie made every visit pleasurable, sharing some of her life stories with me. She recounted coming to America on a 3rd rate ship with nothing but her ratty old mink coat and a hundred dollars left in cash. Greeting her at the dock were Zsa Zsa and Conrad Hilton, Eva and her husband, Richard Brown. She asked her daughters what she could do with her remaining $100. Eva said perhaps it could buy a nice hat, so Jolie went back on board and gave it to the deck hands, who had been so nice to her on the voyage.

Zsa Zsa & Jolie conspired to acquire a new mink for mama. Zsa Zsa's Chinchilla was insured for big bucks. At Radio City Music Hall, they purposely left their coats on their seats, while they visited the ladies room. Upon return they discovered the Chinchilla was still there. Jolie's ratty uninsured mink was gone. So much for larceny!

Eva was the truly talented one. I will never forget my first experience meeting this gorgeous creature. My friend, Bill Traylor, was appearing on Broadway in a play called Nude with Violin starring its author (Private Lives, Blight Spirit) Noel Coward & Eva Gabor. Backstage after the play, Bill introduced me to Mr. Coward an icon in theater, who kindly included me with his cast at the supper party he was hosting at Luchows. The limousine he had ordered would not hold an extra person. So Mr. Coward said, "Miss Lee and I will follow you in a cab." Oh Lord! I was thunderstruck. A Broadway play, a five-star restaurant and riding with the world- famous Noel Coward. Be still my heart! (No matter how I played my cards, I never could've been Mrs. Noel Coward.)

Supper was memorable, but my dessert came via Eva when she said, "Dahhling Rutahh, you are beautiful, adorable, charming, talented and gorgeous. You look exactly like me!" Through the years we became good friends and she shared many of her stories as well. I love the incident at her Palm Springs home. Eva was an avid tennis player and liked her body to look tanned in tennis whites, but never her face or hands. So to even out tan lines on her body, she was laying naked on a floating raft in her pool. Naked, except for a big, veiled sun hat and sunglasses covering her face, little white gloves on her lotion slathered hands. She knew early on how aging the sun could be.

She suddenly had the feeling that she was being observed. Lifting the brim of her big hat and lowering her sunglasses, she discovered way up on a telephone pole, a line man who waved and shouted, "Hi Eva!" Quickly she replied, "No dahhling, Zsa Zsa! As she put it, "Let him think this big fat ass is Zsa Zsa's!

Angie/Eva/Ruta...enjoying being blonde at Eva's
Star Ceremony

My husband Webb got to know both Zsa Zsa and Eva and fell under their spell, as well. One of his proudest moments was escorting Paula Kent Meehan (RedKen founder), Eva and myself around Vegas for dinner and shows. In the casino he bought each of us a big roll of quarters. He said, "Make this last ladies!" (That's my Diamond Jim!")

Eva died too young. She was at her stepdaughter's casita in Baja, California, where she took a fall. She mistakenly assumed that she had only bruised her hip when it was actually fractured. After a day or two the pain was so intense, she was flown to LA and hospitalized where she died of pneumonia. Oh what a loss. The world is a little dimmer without the warm glow of Eva. Zsa Zsa too is no longer with us. I have friends who had been invited and caught a glimpse of her in her bedroom during so-called birthday parties that her " un -PRINCI-pled " husband threw. The Prince was always basking in her dimming limelight and publicity. He too was one of several who claimed paternity of Anna Nicole Smith's daughter. He also offered himself as a candidate for Mayor of LA. However, I must add he took exceptionally good care of Zsa Zsa. Alex Trebek and I visited her shortly before her passing and witnessed his tender care. Bravo Fredrich. Zsa Zsa always claimed George Sanders was the love of her life, but Rubirosa was the best lover.

Hungary that gave us the Gabors also gave us Mitzi Gaynor. What a darling funny and talented girl.

When I was an usherette at Grauman's Chinese Theater, I watched her on the screen and I dreamed of being like her. Mitzi could do it all and still can. Mitzi bought a brand-new Eldorado Convertible every year and at the end of the year, I would buy it from her. It was good for everybody. I wish we were still doing that.

Along with Mitzi, one of the musical queens I enjoyed knowing was June Haver. She was blond, talented and very sweet. What a blessing that both these ladies I admired so much became my good friends.

Speaking of good friends, Debbie Reynolds, was more to me then even a sister could be. It started with *The Thalians*, when Debbie, as President, recognized I was a doer, not a talker. We have shared so much in our lives, good and bad. Debbie would be the first to admit that she had great taste in girlfriends and lousy taste in husbands. Debbie adored my Webb, she claimed she married her last disaster of a husband because he look liked Webb. Sorry sister!

She survived really rotten times, but the auctions of her incredible Hollywood collection more than made up for the debts her lousy husbands brought her. Bravo sister! How sad she did not live long enough to enjoy sharing and spending it.

At the time of her death, I was at our Casita in Las Hadas Mexico. That Christmas was a festive holiday get together for George and Erin Pennacchio, Scotty and Brian, Roni Miller and Gary Damsker and, of course, Webb and me.

We gathered for dinner, a farewell to the holiday week, on the Embarcadero, at which time Scott and George took me aside to tell me the horrible news of Debbie's and Carrie's deaths. George asked if I could muster the energy to say a few words for ABC about my best friend. As I stood numbly on the wharf, a burst of energy and love moved my spirit and the 30 seconds I had expected to fill became at least 30 minutes. George later told me we were live on ABC 7 via Facebook, the whole time and we had over 400,000 views.

A day or 2 later I got word from Debbie's son, Todd, that an at home memorial gathering for the girls was to be held the following Thursday with the Forest Lawn Funeral Friday. I had to be there !!! Panic set in. Try as I may I could not get a flight from Manzanillo to Los Angeles. Sold out for weeks. My pals had already returned home to LA and I was at a loss as to what to do. I accidentally butt dialed Roni at 4 a.m. (2-hour time difference.) Awakened, she thought what the hell I'll give Alaska Airlines another try and magically, maybe with Debbie's help, secured me a seat to LA and return to Mexico after funeral. Roni saved the day!

Webb remained in Mexico with our house guest, so I asked Debbie's and my buddy, Alex Trebek to come to the Memorial with me. Security at the house was tighter than Fort Knox. It never occurred to me to put Alex on the list, which created a small problem. Todd to the rescue.

Debbie – Ruta – Bosom Buddies singing for
Mame (Angela Lansbury)

This was a star filled event. George Lucas, Penny
Marshall, Meg Ryan, Richard Dreyfuss, Buck Henry,
Candice Bergen, Gwyneth Paltrow Trisha and Joely Fisher
to name a few. Alex and I sat with Debbie's lifelong,
beloved, essential right and left hands... Margie Duncan

and Donald Light. Eulogies were delivered by Billie Lourd, Carrie's daughter, and several other amazing speakers...so eloquent!

However even though it was a salute to both mother and daughter, as I recall only lovely Meryl Streep even mentioned Debbie. And beautifully, I must add. These were mostly Carrie's friends, but without Debbie there would be no Carrie. I was heartsick at the lack of deserved esteem for my dearest friend.

Todd asked me to speak at the next day Funeral at Forest Lawn. I thought I would sing an appropriate song, expecting this would take place in the Chapel equipped with piano/organ for accompaniment. Upon arrival much to my surprise, the entire service was held outside at the entombment site. Once again, I think Debbie played guardian angel as her forever brilliant conductor, arranger, Joey Singer, accompanied me on Debbie's "Singing Nun" guitar that Todd has brought to the funeral. It was a painful but precious moment singing her favorites as a goodbye.

Several months later Todd Fisher produced the most extraordinary and gratifying theatrical event at Forest Lawn's big auditorium honoring his mother Debbie and sister Carrie. Ziegfeld could not have created a more beautiful farewell salute. Dancing...singing...great film clips...and amazing, amusing speakers. Yours truly included.

A few years earlier, much to our surprise (Debbie didn't do funerals) she attended the one for our beloved mutual friend Paula Kent Meehan. She loved what I said and sang at the service, took me aside and made me promise that when the time came, I'd do exactly the same for her. Promise fulfilled Debbie, with deepest love.

Anne Jeffreys remains forever a classy lady, who was a real nighttime gal, never rising before the crack of noon. Most of America will know her from the series, Topper, with her husband, Robert Sterling. Anne also did it all, from Broadway to movies and with such pizzazz.

The singing cowboy star Gene Autry had a special place in everyone's heart. This entertainment giant was also made a financial giant by his wife Jackie. She's no lightheaded blonde! I am proud to claim her as one of my best friends. We have been Palm Springs neighbors for many years. I often look to her for financial advice. Maybe someday I'll be a rich as her beloved husband Gene,(Rudolph the Red Nosed Reindeer) Autry...and as philanthropic as the great lady herself. Bravo Jackie Autry for being the force behind so many civic and social projects. The Autry Western Museum is a highlight in any Los Angeles visit.

Beautiful columnist and TV host Toni Holt Kramer and I have had a truly loving friendship for over 50 years. We co-hosted Talk of The Town, a celebrity interview show. It aired across the nation for 5 years. Our producer, Gloria Gebbia was another smart and beautiful blonde. In fact, our company was titled "Blondes have More Fun Productions," and we did!!! Our show was sponsored by Stockcross/Siebert Financial. And by the way their whiz

Andrew McDonald, our Thalians Board member, handles the finances for *The Thalians* and all my Stocks and Bonds as well. Talk of The Town covered major red-carpet events. Being considered celebrities ourselves and personal friends to most Hollywood stars , we snagged extraordinary interviews and scoops. We always stood on the red carpet...not behind press barricades. Often major networks would extend their sound apparatus and use our conversations with stars like Tom Cruise, Arnold Schwarzenegger and Bob Hope. Toni is the hard- working Founder of The Trumpettes supporting President Donald Trump's efforts for America. She lives in Bel Air and Palm Springs California as well as Palm Beach where she creates a glamorous star-studded gala ever year, at Mar a Lago saluting America.

Everybody's favorite *Brady Bunch* mom, Florence Henderson, was probably the most recognized face in America. She was a truly gifted singer, dancer, performer and one of the best salespeople in the business. To top it off, she had a heart bigger and warmer than her delicious smile.

Ann Jillian photo by Wayne Williams – Beyond
being beautiful, glamorous and talented, Annie
is one helluva mother and friend

Ann Jillian, Broadway's gorgeous *Sugar Babies* star, CBS
series - *It's a Living* star- and a glowing film Mae West to
name but a few of her vast credits, is also my beautiful
Lithuanian sister. When needed Ann generously

performed for Thalians and City of Hope. Ann put her booming career aside to be an at home mom when her son Andrew was born. She remains a brilliant singer, performer and headline speaker for The American Cancer Society. She, husband Andy and I are family and share many laugh filled hours at every and any opportunity.

While on beautiful blondes another lovely singer, performer and girlfriend is Broadway's Constance Towers. She can do it all and proved it performing official duties as wife to handsome John Gavin, President Reagan's Ambassador to Mexico. She charmed theater audiences, world-wide government officials and continues to charm daytime fans of General Hospital.

Ruta and Toni Holt Kramer turned the tables
and interviewed Jay

Adorable Connie Stevens is as pretty today as when I first met her some 60 years ago. She's a triple threat performer, make that quadruple, as she is the savvy businesswoman behind Forever Spring beauty products which was a top seller on Home Shopping Network for many years. Bravo Connie.

Before she became the Partridge Family mom, Shirley Jones wowed America with *Oklahoma, Carousel, Music Man* and by winning the Oscar for *Elmer Gantry.* Not only exquisitely beautiful Shirley is one of the most generous and charitable performers I know.

Lovely Laura McKenzie is the "Travel Queen." She hosts the most beautiful travel shows. Having a world-wide audience makes her a formidable presence when she walks into a hotel or hot spot anywhere. Heels click, everyone jumps to attention doing their best. Gorgeous Laura, on the other hand, is the most down home, relaxed, unassuming lady I know. She and husband David have been top notch financial friends and patrons to *The Thalians* with countless productions of shows.

Mamie Van Doren somewhere in her 80's is still a gorgeous blonde bombshell. She's always fun to be with and can give delicious, lurid descriptions of every Hollywood leading man...

That takes me directly to Church and my "church ladies!!!" Singer extraordinaire Helen Grayco, widow of Spike Jones is well into her 90's, looking like she is in her 40's. She does it all with a fresh young attitude. That same attitude is part of Joanie St. Claire's joie de vivre. It is a great compliment to her work as one of our foremost interior designers. We see each other at Mass and brunches that follow...hence I call these adorable, sexy women my church ladies.

Speaking of church ladies, I must include another interior design maven from Canada, Margrit Mortensen. She is my neighbor and loving friend in Las Hadas, Mexico. She beautifies everyone's life with her style and LOVE.

Lest I forget...my Temple lady Francine Goldberg. We have been like sisters for over 40 years. Francine is the real estate queen of Manzanillo. The one you must go to for a beautiful property in Mexico.

The last, but certainly not least, the late Phyllis Diller, continues to color my life. I will never forget her comment that topped my comment about owing my career to BF Goodrich, as foam rubber bust pads were sometimes essential. She commented, "Ruta you've worn so much rubber in your bra, you've erased what little tits you had." Above and beyond the laughter she brought us, she was a loving friend. She once said, "I've converted everything in my life into love, which she happily shared with Webb and me." Wow! ... did she ever. She filled our lives generously with love and laughter.

Seasons Picture

Chapter 16

Animal "Tails"

Aside from snakes, I don't think there's any animal that I've ever been afraid of. Webb was quick to say that if I ran into a tiger, in the jungle, I'd probably get down on my knees and say, "Here kitty kitty" ... and adopt it. He's right. I think animals can sense when they're loved. I'm not sure snakes can. I have a morbid fear of snakes and dentists and I'm not sure in which order. I tried to get past my fear of snakes by forcing myself to walk around the quadrangle snake house at the San Diego zoo. The covered arcade is about 15 feet wide and the first lap I walked as far away from the glass enclosures as possible. By lap four, I was able to get fairly close, but to this day, I still shudder at the picture of a snake even in a book and slam it shut. I'm still not fond of dentists either!

My self-induced snake therapy must have worked, as I was able to touch my friend's pet boa constrictor. Much to my surprise, it wasn't scaly feeling at all. It felt like a hard rubber tire. Nevertheless, not my idea of a great pet.

Coming home one evening with girlfriend Carmen in tow, I started to step out of my car to open the garage door.(before garage door openers) I heard a rustle at my feet, jumped back in, slamming my door shut, screaming, "There's a snake!" To Carmen's surprise, I raced the car back and forth, back and forth, back and forth, all the time terrified, that the snake would climb through the exhaust pipe. I finally turned the car and headlights on the varmint and said to Carmen, "You get out and see if it's dead." She picked it up by the tail and said, "It's dead alright, you killed your belt."

We are a household of pets, four dogs, 3 cats, a bird ... make that a hundred hummingbirds and several families of deer that come to drink the water we provide. To say nothing of the raccoons, possums and skunks that occasionally stop by.

I didn't have a lot of pets when I was kid. We had a pair of rabbits that we kept down in the basement and need I say, how upset I was when I found out we ate them. Everything tastes like chicken. Later in life I discovered rattle snake taste like chicken too.

When I was kid , a dog wandered on to our property and I claimed him as my own. Then he ran away; I looked for him for two weeks, crying the whole time. I didn't realize that he had just gone back to his actual owners. My mother, seeing the agony I went though said, "No more pets."

Around the age of 6 or 7, I discovered a treasure trove of coins that had fallen out of people's pockets and slipped between the sofa cushions. I then checked diligently every day and managed to collect a dollar or two in quarters and dimes. Without saying anything, I bought a puppy from someone on the street. I brought it back saying, "Look what followed me home!" I took the puppy to stay the summer with me at my aunt's farm in

Colborne, Ontario. Of course, having bought the puppy on the street, I didn't know that it was sick, and it died that summer. We had a little burial ceremony, a practice that I continue to this day.

Later, in Hollywood, after I'd made a few dollars in movies, I bought what every girl dreams of having, a tiny toy poodle. I named him Yoyo because he looked like one on his leash. He was probably one of the best pets I ever had. I took him everywhere. We had him for many years and when he became extremely ill and it was time to put him down, it was torturous. But it was also the first time where I saw a vet help my pet to an easy death, without further suffering. I've been through that many times now and I've had to recognize that dogs don't live as long as we humans. If we get 10 or 15 years of joy from our pups, then we have to be grateful.

I have four dogs now of varying ages, all rescues. One of them was a "$20,000 rescue." At "SHARE" a celebrity charity event, my best friend Margie Petersen was bidding against American Idol's Nigel Lythgoe for a poodle puppy, donated by the dog whisperer Cesar Millan. At Margie's 20 K bid, Nigel was out-bid. Her older Yorkie, Sassy, would not tolerate the new puppy, so Margie begged me to take it (ha-ha GLADLY). The dog came with Cesar's training, but let me tell you, the dog has been with us now for more than five years and she is still untrained, but she's so sweet and beautiful, who cares.

I encourage animal adoptions, though I have discovered the hard way that sometimes it can be an unnecessarily tough process. I can only speak from the bad experiences I've had with one-breed shelters. These shelters are run by well-intended people, who sometimes would rather keep the dogs in pens than give them to a home that doesn't meet, in their opinion, the stiff criteria. I applied to one of these rescue shelters, to find a replacement for my little Yorkie Yogi. Their site pictured many available Yorkies. I would take one, two or more. I had to fill out papers that are far more extensive and personal than applications for citizenship. Well, we filled out these papers to completion. Weeks went by. After about three unanswered calls and emails, I persisted to see what was going on. I said, "Are you going to give us those puppies?"

They said, "No, because you're an older couple and these are young dogs." I thought, 'Do they not know the math? Do they not know we will far out live those dogs unless we get hit by a bus?' How stupid to keep dogs caged, rather than giving them a wonderful home.

Another time, I adopted a Great Dane from a shelter, a gloriously beautiful dog that I named in honor of my famed Hollywood costume designer, Grady Hunt. He had a huge Rottweiler named Ruta, so I returned the honor by naming the Dane, Grady Hünt. In German, Hünt means dog. The Dane's enormous size prevented me from taking him on the road, while I was doing my shows, five to eight weeks at a time. My mother was in charge of our menagerie, while I was away.

One of my beloved Danes, Spike – 200 lbs. of love with his
mate and puppies

These were the days before we had flea preventatives, like
Advantage and such. We live in the hills, so of course there are
fleas. My mother would put the dog out in his compound

during the day and bring him in at night. While I was gone, these shelter people dropped in without notice to visit the dog. They literally confiscated the dog, taking him out of his huge play area, because he had some fleas and took him back to the shelter, placing him in a small pen. Upon my return, I fought to get my best friend back. In spite of letters from the mayor, council members and other prominent citizens, the shelter would not return the dog. Grady, pining for me, was naturally upset and must've been provoked, as they accused my gentle giant of attacking a handler. They put him down. My heart was broken. I didn't like those "self-righteous, S.O.B.'s."

However, I have been blessed with my latest adoptions from the wonderful Shelter Hope Pets in Thousand Oaks, CA. My 3-pound pup Mousie is the princess in our household. Not long ago my gal pal Jackie Rosenberg called and said "I just adopted Tulip from your Shelter ...hurry up and get her sister Daisy." They are both amazing Yorkie, Chihuahua mixes...don't know to call them Chorkies or Yorkie-huahuas.

I urge people to adopt a dog. Hell, adopt two; they keep each other company. Dogs are such a gift to us ... OR are they just so smart that they know how to manipulate us humans. After all, we feed, shelter and take care of them and most of them don't have to work for a living, like we do. Let's face it, statistics have shown that people who have animals have better lives. They live longer, calmer and happier because of animals.

I also have a love for exotic animals. Years ago, when I was working at Paramount, the animal wrangler on John Wayne's movie *Hatari* came to me and said, "You love animals Ruta. Have you got a place for a baby elephant?" They were trying to find a home for the little guy. I was tempted to take and keep him in my backyard. Can you see me now, shoveling elephant poop? I regretfully declined, knowing it would outgrow our space here.

Lucille Ball and I rode elephants for *The Thalians* Charity opening night of the Circus. I said rode... make that straddled...ouch... elephant hairs are wiry.

Ruth and Kent Perkins – Rhett Turner – Debbie and
Jo Anne Worley – best friends all

Elephants are interesting and smart creatures. Years ago, Webb and I were in Thailand with Ruth Buzzi and her husband Kent. We went to a big zoological park where there was an elephant show. These big elephants would come tromping in and run around the amphitheater. They asked for volunteers to demonstrate that elephants don't actually step on people. Kent Perkins volunteered Ruth who's fearless. So she found herself lying on the ground with tons of elephants stepping over her. Suddenly she thought, 'What am I doing? I'm out of my mind!' She got up and scurried out of the ring. I'm not sure she ever forgave her husband or any of us for cheering her on.

Parrots are wonderful and exotic creatures. When I was a little girl, we had one named Polly (how novel). He was a funny bird that loved butter. He wasn't caged and had free run of the property, returning to his cage at night. The dogs and cats didn't mess with Polly. However, something frightened him and he flew off. The first time he was returned to us by a neighbor, who said Polly helped himself to the butter on their kitchen table. Then something frightened it again one day and he flew away and this time he never returned. We had him for almost 20 years. I just hope he found a good home ...with butter.

We also had a beautiful white peacock. We put him up at night on a perch close to a ceiling so he couldn't stretch his neck to scream. They're great watchdogs and sound like a diesel truck applying air brakes, if they spot something strange.

A coyote got our bird, which surprised me because peacocks can usually fly out of range. The bird was familiar with our dogs and maybe didn't recognize the coyote as a predator.

We now have Sammy, a Golden Crested Cockatoo. Having a bird like this is like having a spoiled three- year-old child for the rest of your life. They are selfish little bastards and as pretty as they are, sometimes they can drive you crazy, just like kids. But he's my sweet bird and he loves me. I think that he's a single person bird. Sammy has learned to emulate what he hears the most. In this house that's barking and laughing. He knows how to do both. When he whines, we move him from his inside cage, (which looks more like an apartment) and put him in his poolside apartment. He's quite amazing. They live long lives, around 100 years. I've made arrangements that at my death, Sammy goes to my Godson Scott Deshong and his partner Brian Theobald. They are going to have to work out who gets Sammy at their deaths.

I'm drawn to other people who share a love for animals. My friend, Elaine Trebek Kares runs a shelter for cats. LA Zoo Board Member, Betty White, of course, has yet to meet an animal that she doesn't like.

Erica Brunson raises money and donates a great deal herself to buy and construct motorized clinics, dedicated to spaying and neutering animals. The streets are filled with non-neutered animals. This means that more pups are brought into the world to suffer. She sends these trucks out into the various neighborhoods and barrios.

Speaking of beauty and beasts. My darling friend Stefanie Powers is the amazing "mother superior" of The William Holden Wildlife Foundation. She has devoted her life to the preservation, education and conservation of the beautiful animals and people of East Kenya through the tireless work of the Foundation. As President and chief fund raiser she proudly states that not one penny raised is used by or for administrators. Their time, travel, work, is their willing contribution to the cause, all honoring the life and work her beloved William Holden.

My late friend, Paula Meehan, founder of Redken hair products, has set up the Pet Care foundation, Pets 90210, and grooming trucks that go to shelters. They wash and fluff up the darling animals, making them pretty and more adoptable. Her products have beautified generations of the humankind. Now she's beautifying the animal world too.

Forever lovely Stefanie Powers

I'm on the board of OFI, the Orangutan Foundation International. It is a fabulous organization, which was formed to preserve the life and habitat of Orangutans in Borneo. They are being killed and deprived of habitat due the deforestation of the area, all for the planting and raising of palm trees for palm oil. There's poaching and incursion on the preserve lands. When mothers are killed, these human-like orangutan babies are left defenseless in desperate need of caring and kindness. OFI under the leadership of Dr. Birute Galdikas, needs our financial and physical help to continue this much needed work.

...A lap full of rescues and love

I really get so upset by any kind of abuse to an animal. Abuse has many forms ... not putting out water and food, not providing shelter, etc. I feel like people were given the sense and ability to care for themselves. Animals that are not in the wild don't have that. It is up to us to take care of something that we have chosen to take out of the wild. It's up to us to be the custodians of what God has put on this earth. We have to care for all living things whether it be humans, plants or animals. I believe more of us should be aware and take that responsibility.

Chapter 17

Shoulda, Coulda, Woulda

I've never been filled with regret. I'm very content with the life I've lived. Besides, I'm generally focused on the present because there's so much yet to do. Of course there are some ***shoulda, coulda woulda's*** that may have made my life different.

For instance, I was doing the TV show *Tempo* with Regis Philbin. Andy Warhol was a guest. He arrived with his very strange, but colorful entourage. After the show, he said, "Ruta, I want you to come to New York with me. I will make you the biggest thing that's ever happened. There's a certain Monroesque quality about you."

I thought 'Do I really want to get involved in his weird world, with all the rumored LSD use?' I was such a goody-two shoes. How was I to know that he would become *the man,* a cultural icon, who turned people around him into icons as well. I guess I ***shoulda***.

Here's another story. Paula Kent Meehan had invited the Pete (astronaut) Conrads, the Bob aka Pete (publisher) Petersens, the Pete (Admiral) Longs, Webb and myself for a cruise on her yacht, around the islands of Fiji. We called them Pete, Pete and Repeat. Malcolm Forbes owned an island in the area Laucala, which was for sale for around four millions dollars. With just the people on the yacht, we **coulda** bought that island. A few years later, it sold for over 10 million.

Malcolm's house was just a beach shack but located on a mountainside with a beautiful pool in front was at that point, not being used. When you looked out to sea you saw reef after reef with the palest green, then turquoise, then blue water. The sugar cane on the hillside was swaying in the breeze. I stood there with our friends and began to sing, 'Born on the opposite side of the sea, we are as different as people can be.'.... singing the songs from *South Pacific* in the South Pacific. The beauty of it all brought us to tears.

Mega- Magazine Publisher - Bob Petersen had sent his *Skin Diver* magazine reporters to do a big feature, which resulted in an enormous boon to the island's economy. So they welcomed Bob like a God. Clearly, we **coulda** and **shoulda** made this our personal heaven on earth.

Actually Margie and Bob were as close to Olympian Gods as mortals may be. He was a handsome self-made zillionaire and she was a beauty queen, humble, yet sassy, rolled into one lovely person. Beauty and wealth do not guarantee a happily ever after life. My dearest friends lost their 2 young sons in a tragic plane crash. I don't think anything is more painful. This put Margie into depression and her bed for an awfully long period.

Her darling Irish housekeeper Nancy would literally bathe and feed her daily. After months of her un-ceasing pain Debbie said. "Ruta I think we should have Margie chair *The Thalians* Ball this year." I was aghast..."Chair the ball...she can't even raise her head off the pillow." My amazingly intuitive Debbie said, "I know dear you'll have to do all the work, but it will get Margie's ass out of bed to at least hold meetings at the house."

Once again Debbie, the girl scout, to the rescue. IT WORKED and brought Margie into the world of the living again. With the help of Gigi Carlton, Mr. Petersen's peerless right hand, who took notes, made suggestions and soothed and smoothed the process, the star-studded event was flawless.

One of the many Thalians galas – Debbie – Margie
Petersen – Whoopie – Bob Petersen and Ruta

This brought a sense of pride and smiles of delight to Margie which was gratifying to see…all thanks to Debbie's insight. Margie and Bob then generously chaired many of our Thalians Galas. Margie and I even resumed our occasional shopping sprees…make that wholesale sprees. We both had worked hard for a living and loved a bargain. The Petersen's were our best chums. Our lives together and our extensive travels are unforgettable. Margie's patron saint is St. Theresa of the Roses. There is not a church in this world that I visited where I have not lit a candle for Margie at Teresa's shrine. I'm sure she and Debbie are asking St. Theresa to keep an eye on me too.

In the 60's and 70's Warner Brothers was the leader in hour-long television shows … everything from *Maverick to 77 Sunset Strip. W*esterns were hot and therefore the primary focus. WB had signed and made big national stars out of numerous young people, including Jim Garner, Efrem Zimbalist, Troy Donahue, Connie Stevens, Clint Walker, etc.

I was fortunate enough to work on all these shows, several times. I became a favorite with the producers and directors because I worked hard, fast and above all had a wild sense of humor. I got paid the top guest salary, which, as I recall, was around $750.00 a week. When I was offered a contract for an upcoming new show at Warners, I politely declined, as the contract salary would've been half of what I was then making as a guest star on their shows. I ***shoulda, coulda*** and if I ***woulda***, the publicity value alone that the studio machine offered was of way more value than the money I would lose. If I

252

woulda, the future fame would have more than made up for the loss of salary.

...from Peter Pan -"I'm flying" which I did a
lot getting to theaters around the country

When Broadway beckoned, I made a big booboo.
Elaine Stritch was leaving the Broadway production

of *Company*, world famous producer, Hal Prince came to Los Angeles to hold auditions. I was one of many who sang for him. In fairly short order, enquiries were made regarding my availability to come to New York. Once again, numbers ruled.

Broadway salaries were very low, compared to television. While I loved the idea of living for a while in New York, in doing the math, I found I couldn't afford it at $400.00 or $500.00 a week. Give up my lovely home, pool, car, friends to live in a hovel, doing 8 shows a week, didn't strike me as a glamorous way to live. In retrospect, I **shoulda** taken any chance offered because in my heart of hearts, I know that I am a true stage animal. My energy and charisma reach out to a theatre audience and Broadway would have recognized that. I've had the joy of playing many Broadway shows all around the country, but never on Broadway.

Speaking of Broadway, I really made a dumb real estate booboo. In the early 60's I met my theater buddy and later director of some Thalian shows, Rudy Tronto when he was cast in the Kansas City Starlight theater production of Peter Pan. We fell into instant friendship. He was Smee, the pirate and Nana the dog. I was Peter. Our opening night in this huge outdoor theater was the night of the first Moon Landing. My oversized flights on the oversized stage had me hoping my landings would be as gentle and successful as Neil Armstrong's.

Back to my boo-boo, At the time Rudy was living in a terrific first level brownstone apartment. It was in the low seventies just off Central Park. The building came up for sale. Great location, huge backyard and 2 upper floor rental apartments. Rudy asked me if I'd be interested as he did not have the cash. $65,000 dollars! Well...in the early sixties that was a helluva lot of money. I worried, pondered and decided I wasn't in New York enough to warrant taking on the financial debt and responsibility. YIKES, that building now would be worth multi multi-millions. I could have been a Manhattan Mogul. Ok, *shoulda, coulda, woulda,* but I didn't, and you know what friends? I'm still damn happy.

Chapter 18

Guardian Angels

Throughout my life, I've often felt guidance and protection from something or someone beyond this realm. Certainly from God and perhaps from those I've loved, who've gone before me. I think that I do get a little help from guardian angels, as I believe in divine intervention.

There are so many reasons why I do. For instance, there was the evening for the City of Hope affiliate dinner. I was an honoree because I had produced many shows for the *Founders For Diabetic Research*. God bless Alex Trebek, Jack Carter, Milton Berle, Anne Jillian and Vikki Carr, all my buddies who came to perform. At this event, the fundraisers from all over the nation, were wined and dined and mingled with celebrities.

After a rewarding and exhausting evening, we were leaving the Hilton and I asked Webb to drive by CBS, so I could pick up a script for *The Bonnie Hunt Show*, which started the next morning. We got the script and drove home. I climbed the stairs while Webb parked the car, my arms loaded with an award, my shoes, script and a goody bag from the event.

As we reached the gated entry at the top of the stairs, we heard from behind us, "Don't turn around or I'll blow your fucking brains out." Well, we automatically turned around and said, "What?" There stood a tall, slim, young black man. I knew he was black because I could see the color of his hands. I could also see the color of the big automatic he was holding. He had a mask on his face and his hat was pulled down. In a soft Johnny Mathis voice that belied his actions, he said, "I told you not to turn around. Put your hands up. Drop everything."

It was one of those nights where I had worn crappy dangling earrings, good bracelets, a good watch and a very good ring.

The ring was important to me, so as he said take everything off, I did and dropped the ring in the bushes. He got the stuff in his hands and said to Webb, "Now give me yours. Take off your watch." Then he said to me, "Where's the **rock**?" Now I don't know if he saw it when I put my hands up, or whether he knew about the rock. Did he follow us home from the hotel?

All of these things were going my mind, as we're standing here at the gate that we haven't opened yet. Even though it was an important ring, it was not worth dying over. I said, "Well, I don't know. I must have dropped it. I'm nervous. You're scaring the hell out of me." I found the ring and I gave it to him.

He said, "Now, we're going inside to your safe. You make one peep; you are going to be dead." I knew if we went inside, anything could happen. Are the freaking dogs even barking? No, not a sound from them! I said, "Look, we don't have a safe." .... which we don't. "What you don't understand is, I work for *Home*

Shopping Network and we sell phony jewelry. You're welcome to everything."

Before he could question anything, my guardian angel came into play and told me to say, "Webb, Webb, I'm fainting" ... and I collapsed to the ground. I fell in such a way I could still see what was going on. I was acting of course. As he went down the stairs, he said, "If you call the cops, I'll come back and blow up your fucking house."

I ran through the gate and to a window where I could see the bottom of the driveway. I saw lights on the street. An old car pulled up, but I couldn't really tell the color. We called the police, but the robbers were already long gone before anyone arrived.

Till this day, I still feel violated and angry. For some time after, our homecomings were like the raid on Entebbe. I'd have a gun. Webb would have a gun. We'd cover each other. The solution was to install a security lighting system everywhere.

What I remembered is that a young man, tall slim, very soft-spoken, was bagging my groceries at *Ralphs and* commented on my beautiful ring. I responded that my husband worked hard for it. He likely gave signals to accomplices in the parking lot.

I remember all of this, because one of our tenants was down on the lower level of our driveway, as I was coming home from the grocery store. He said that I was followed by two men in a car, who turned and left when they saw him. I think that was the connection to my robbery. They had spotted the **rock**. I think it was also an interception by my guardian angels. I can only hope that whoever got the proceeds of my ring needed it a hell of a lot more than I did. And now if anyone comments on my jewelry, I say, "Thank you, these Cubic Zirconia's are wonderful."

Ladies be aware, shopping or parking, as follow-home robberies are still prevalent.

I figured out a long time ago that if anybody ever came up that driveway after me, my guardian angels and I would put the car into reverse and slam them so hard it would shove them into the street. Gratefully, I've never had to do that.

That same driveway came into play once again with my guardian angels. I say angels because I move so fast it takes more than one to take care of me. On a rare rainy California evening I was racing home from work to throw myself into a gown to attend one more black-tie awards evening. I had told my date to go to the event and I would catch up as fast as I could. In the pouring rain, I hurriedly got into my car, drove down the driveway and for some then unknown reason, stopped and waited at the bottom of the drive for several long seconds. As I became aware that I was losing precious time, a fifteen-foot cement wall collapsed into Laurel Canyon, mere inches from where I was sitting. Had I not stopped for that unknown reason I would have been under tons of cement. Thank you my guardian angels. And boy, did I keep them busy.

The next close call was during the production of South Pacific for the San Bernardino Civic Light Opera. After the comedy number Honey Bun, I was backstage, lying on the Emile DeBecque set coffee table, catching my breath. Lying there, breathing deeply. High above me I watched hanging sandbag weights softly moving with the air currents. Once again, for some unknown reason, I got up just as a sandbag came crashing down through the table I had been laying on. Once again, thank you guardian angels.

At Warner Brothers *77 Sunset Strip* stage I was watching the action being shot from the director's tall chair. While I was quite comfortable and had been invited to use that chair, I once again got that strange feeling that I should move. Just as I did, a klieg light fell from the catwalk and crushed the chair to smithereens. Friends, all I can say is when you hear that inner voice, take heed. Your angels are speaking.

While I'm speaking of guardian angels, I salute and thank my Lithuanian live-in cousin Ona Katilius for being my live guardian angel/ major domo of my life.

Ona Katilius – My Life blessing

Chapter 19

This House is a Home - The Tapestry of Life

Barbara Stewart and Dick Gautier Wedding –
Robert Vaughn gave her away – Peter Marshall
was Best Man and I was Maid of Honor

For over 50 years, my Hollywood Hills house has been an architectural Prima Donna. It's been the cover story in many home and garden style magazines and television shows. The almost 100-year-old palazzo has even been the setting for many interviews, for my *Talk of the Town* and *Lifestyles* TV Shows.   We once made the terrible mistake of allowing it to be used for a Roger Corman film (oy what repairs). Handsome and prolific as he is, the SOB never hired me to be in any of his movies.

Most gratifying is when the place has been dolled up for the many beautiful weddings held in it. I've often thought that if I couldn't continue earning a living in show business, I could do it in the wedding business.

My Goddaughter Diana (Carmen's child) was married to Randy Hill here, followed by my Goddaughter Maryte and her U.S. Marine Husband, Greg Coleman. Maryte is the young cousin I struggled for many years to get out of the Soviet Union. I'm blessed to call her my daughter. She's incredible , a true gift from God that is beside me through good and bad times.

A standout Hollywood wedding was that of Barbara, "Gomer Pyle" Stuart and Dick "Bye Bye Birdie" Gautier, with Peter "Hollywood Squares" Marshall as best man and me as bride's maid , with Robert "Man from Uncle" Vaughn, acting as father of the bride. It was a star-studded ceremony and reception, all covered by Rona Barrett. Sorry to say Barbara's honeymoon was spent in the hospital as the next day she wound up there with a blood clot. When she got past that, married life and honeymoon resumed.

This wonderful house is on a 6-acre compound with several guesthouses that are rental properties. Remember, I learned the lesson well. Own property, rent it, and let the tenants help pay the mortgage.

Being a landlady is rewarding, but oh boy, can it be challenging. Not all tenants are God sent. I have been left with premises that looked like it had been through a war. These little surprises are always a financial and emotional burden. However, let's not speak of those. Rather ... let's speak of sweet rental remembrances.

Some of my celebrity tenants included Family Affair's Brian Keith (handsome, tidy, rent always on time), *Beverly Hillbillies*, Max Bear Jr., darling but left an awful mess. I almost had the Jackson family, as Jermaine wanted one of the bungalows. However, I panicked at the thought of the entire canyon resounding with the Jackson beat and the complaints that would be engendered.

One horrific experience was renting to what we thought was a quality gentleman, only to discover much to our chagrin that he was running a hillside whorehouse. The ongoing traffic was our big clue. We extinguished his red light with an eviction notice. I must say he did pay the rent on time.

Other rental properties include town houses in Fort Worth, Texas, a Penthouse at Las Hadas, in Manzanillo Mexico. The movie 10 with Julie Andrews, Dudley Moore and the lovely Bo Derek was shot there, a true Mexican paradise.

Another paradise is Palm Springs where I bought my first house when I was very young with the idea of renting it to pay the mortgage. I had worked with Gene Kelly at *The Thalians* when we honored him. I also played his

265

lover in *Marjorie Morningstar,* so it was fun to rent him my little Palm Springs House and even more fun to say Gene Kelly slept in my bed. Others, who slept in that bed include the adorable Artie Johnson (Laugh-In), Jack Cassidy, then married to Shirley Jones and Bill Orr, then the head of Warner Brothers Television ... to name a few.

As you can see friends, we have houses everywhere. I guess you could say, "I sleep around." The only problem is I never know where I need sugar or where I need toilet paper.

I did a lot growing up in the main Los Angeles house. It had once belonged to Rita Hayworth and Orson Wells. I constantly envision her descending the stairs. I keep rubbing my ass on the walls hoping some of Rita's glamour will cling.

My home has housed many friends in their early struggles that have gone on to become whizzes in theater and in business. My longtime Fort Worth hairdresser David Blackstock, (cousin to Reba McEntire), lived here for a long time. He calls me his *fairy Godmother* and himself, the *fairy Godson*. My other Godson Scott Deshong also was a resident, for some time, when he first came to Hollywood. He is now a whiz with a major celebrity law firm and a great asset in my life. His partner Brian Theobald is in property management and is my go-to man with all property issues and thank God, also serves as my computer guru.

My blood related family is very small. I do have some really nifty cousins in the Boston area, the Bumilias. Cousin Susan Trautman has a fabulous catering service. Parties Perfect does the best lobster dinners I have ever had.

Closer to home, my childhood friend, precious cousin Lily Dutch is like myself, an only child, She, however, has given me two God children.

Godson, Paul Dutch, married to a gorgeous Filipina, Abby, is in the funeral/cremation and water filtration and real estate business. So, I'm covered on all bases.

His sister, Alyson Dutch, my Goddaughter, did a lot of growing up in this house as well. I, who never had children, took on the challenge of a difficult 16-year-old girl. She learned discipline and developed a strong work ethic. Alyson now lives in Malibu, where she has a thriving public relations firm. Hell, maybe someday I'll move in with her.

I am truly blessed with all of these children and their partners. They are my kids and as always say, I got them without birthing pains or stretch marks.

Having this property has paid off in more ways than just financially. Girls trust me, don't go for diamonds, go for real estate. It's like a cow that never runs dry.

A toast to my fabulous kids – Brian Theobald –
Paul Dutch – Marite Coleman – Alyson Dutch -
Scott Deshong

My life has been blessed with so many wonderful
experiences and relationships. Family and friends that
have made my memories are all part of who I am today.
Some of these dear ones are still in my life. Others have
gone on to their greater reward. Regardless, I know that
we are all still connected.

I believe we are all part of a beautiful fabric that God has
woven ... a *tapestry of life. E*ach of us is a thread in this
tapestry. Some threads are golden or silver, some plain,

some rough. But, we all have our place within this great universal design. Even when people pass on, I believe they are still connected to this fabric. Their legacy may be picked up by another thread and continues on.

I didn't really think about any of this, until I had to eulogize someone. That's when it all became crystal clear to me that we're never entirely separated from each other.

We are all woven into something greater than ourselves... all part of the wonderful tapestry of life.

Thanks for taking this drive with me. I've shared memories that I saw in the rearview mirror. I hope you've enjoyed them. If you've been part of my life and you can't find yourself mentioned here, blame the editor; you've wound up on the cutting room floor.

All I can do now is wish us a lovely continuing journey into the future with the surprises that come with each turn. I hope our guardian angels are with us all the way in the now and the hereafter. I'm not here to teach you a damn thing, but I do urge you to live your life to the fullest. It's the only one you've got (unless you're Shirley MacLaine). Let's meet again at the next rest stop. I love you and I'm grateful, so please, please...Consider Your Ass Kissed!

Oooooh - P.S.

A thousand kisses go to two profoundly special people, earthly guardian angels. My Texas pal and extraordinary public relations guru Barry Rogers, whose constant urging finally made me sit down with him and record my memories. I talked, he taped, transcribed and typed. Whew!

And Judy Diamond, my beloved personal redhead, assistant, researcher who waded through reams of material with me and was a constant pain (in the place that's kissed) until we got it done.

And the amazing Harlan Boll for using his vast knowledge and PR expertise in getting my turkey to the presses/table so we can all enjoy the feast.

Ruta – Barry Rogers – Judy Diamond – The 3 Musketeers trying to make order of my life.

...and Webb, xxx, goodnight Handsome

Ruta Lee's

Film, TV
and
Stage Roles

Title	Role	Notes
Adventures of Superman	Teenager	Episode: "My Friend Superman" Credited as Rita Kilmonis
Schlitz Playhouse of Stars	Various roles	2 episodes
Burns and Allen	Various roles	2 episodes
Lux Video Theatre	Marion	Episode: "I'll Never Love Again"
Science Fiction Theatre	Student	Episode: "The Unexplored"
Alfred Hitchcock Presents	Various roles	Episodes: "Whodunit", "The Cheney Vase"
I Led Three Lives	Louise Burke	Episode: "New Member"
Dragnet		Episode: "The Big Daughter"
Highway Patrol	Lea Franklin	Episode: "Armored Car"
Suspicion	Betty	Episode: "The Story of Marjorie Reardon"
Captain David Grief	Rose	Episode: "The Affair at Les Trois Magots"
Maverick	Various roles	3 episodes
The Lineup	Various roles	8 episodes
The Gray Ghost		Episode: "Contraband"
Playhouse 90		Episode: "The Right Hand Man"
The Walter Winchell File	Joan	Episode: "The Dice of Fortune: File #34"
Mickey Spillane's Mike Hammer	Various roles	2 episodes
Man with a Camera	Dolly MacDermott	Episode: "Second Avenue Assassin"
Rescue 8	Ann Dagget	Episode: "The Cage"
December Bride	Carol Hodges	Episode: "Bride's Father-in-Law"

Title	Role	Notes
Sugarfoot	Various roles	2 episodes
M Squad	Various roles	3 episodes
Gunsmoke	Various roles	2 episodes
77 Sunset Strip	Various roles	5 episodes
Perry Mason	Various roles	5 episodes
Yancy Derringer	Romilly Vale	Episode: "Two of a Kind"
The Restless Gun	Lucy Collins	Episode: "The Painted Beauty"
Peter Gunn	Marie Gipson	Episode: "Edie Finds a Corpse"
The Millionaire	Angela Temple	Episode: "Millionaire Angela Temple"
Richard Diamond, Private Detective	Louise	Episode: "Jukebox"
Bat Masterson	Nellie Fontana	Episode: "The Death of Bat Masterson"
Alcoa Theatre	Emily Meadows	Episode: "Medals for Harry"
The Lawless Years	Gloria Fallon	Episode: "The Payoff"
Markham	Tammy Miles	Episode: "The Duelists"
Johnny Staccato	Dee Dee	Episode: "The Naked Truth"
Tightrope	Laura	Episode: "Stand on Velvet"
Whirlybirds	Ginny	Episode: "Mr. Jinx"
Hennesey	Ruth Thomas	Episode: "Hennesey and Peyton Place"
The Man from Blackhawk	Ginnie Thompson	Episode: "The Legacy"
United States Marshal	Various roles	4 episodes
The Alaskans	Various roles	2 episodes
Colt .45	Various roles	2 episodes

Title	Role	Notes
Wagon Train	Various roles	2 episodes
Shotgun Slade	Lilly Cody	Episode: "Killer's Brand"
The Rebel	Ellen Barton	Episode: "Grant of Land"
Hawaiian Eye	Various roles	3 episodes
The Tab Hunter Show		Episode: "Turnabout"
Michael Shayne	Naomi Lester	Episode: "Spotlight On a Corpse"
Dante	Peggy Braddock	Episode: "Dante's Fickle Fate"
The Brothers Brannagan	Lynn	Episode: "Shot in the Dark"
The Case of the Dangerous Robin		Episode: "Brink of Disaster"
Zane Grey Theater	Jenny Aldrich	Episode: "Man from Everywhere"
Harrigan and Son	Rose	Episode: "The Legacy"
Stagecoach West	Various roles	2 episodes
Laramie	Opal Crane	Episode: "Siege at Jubilee"
The Outlaws	Jennie	Episode: "Farewell Performance"
Poor Mr. Campbell	Priscilla Edwards	Television film
Gunsmoke	Jenny Glover	Episode: "Jenny" aired 13 October 1962
Cheyenne	Lenore Walton Hanford	Episode: "Wanted for the Murder of Cheyenne Bodie"
The Dick Powell Show	Eva Gobel	Episode: "Crazy Sunday"
Rawhide	Various roles	2 episodes
The Andy Griffith Show	Andy on Trial as Jean Boswell, The Hollywood Party as Darlene Mason	2 episodes

Title	Role	Notes
Bonanza	Rita Marlowe	Episode: "A Woman Lost"
Arrest and Trial	Colleen Riley	Episode: "Call It a Lifetime"
The Twilight Zone	Flora Gordon	Episode: "A Short Drink from a Certain Fountain"
Temple Houston	Lucy Tolliver	Episode: "Enough Rope"
Fractured Flickers	Herself	Episode 20
The Travels of Jaimie McPheeters	Zoe Pigalle	Episode: "The Day of the Lame Duck"
The Fugitive	Mrs. Janet Loring	Episode: "Angels Travel on Lonely Roads: Part 2"
The Virginian	Various roles	2 episodes
Burke's Law	Various roles	3 episodes
The Bill Dana Show	Yvette Renay	Episode: "Beauty and the Bellhop"
Gomer Pyle, U.S.M.C.	Gloria Morgan	Episode: "Gomer Dates a Movie Star"
The Wackiest Ship in the Army		Episode: "The Stowaway"
The Wild Wild West	Various roles	2 episodes
The Lucy Show	Miss Audrey Fields; herself	Episodes: "Lucy's Substitute Secretary"; "Lucy Meets the Berles"
Judd, for the Defense	Alida Nye	Episode: "To Love and Stand Mute"
Mannix	Jean Coleman	Episode: "Run, Sheep, Run"
Hogan's Heroes	Various roles	3 episodes
Ironside	Marian	Episode: "To Kill a Cop"

Title	Role	Notes
The Guns of Will Sonnett	Fan	Episode: "Trail's End"
The Flying Nun	Faye/Sister Mary Grace	2 episodes
Marcus Welby, M.D.	Shirley Ballinger	Episode: "All Flags Flying"
Love, American Style	Various roles	3 episodes
Mayberry R.F.D.	Terry Phillips	Episode: "The City Planner"
A Howling in the Woods	Sharon	Television film
The Mod Squad	Gloria Hardy	Episode: "Exit the Closer"
Arnie	Miss Fletcher	Episode: "Et Tu, Arnie"
Me and the Chimp	Lavelle Wiggins	Episode: "My Pet, the Thief"
Match Game	Guest Panelist	One Week
High Rollers	Co-Hostess	Daytime
Indict and Convict	Phyllis Dorfman	Television film
Roll, Freddy, Roll!	Evelyn Danton Kane	Television film
Mork & Mindy	Lisa	Episode: "Mork's Night Out"
Three's Company	Various roles	2 episodes
The Flintstone Comedy Show	Hidea Frankenstone (Voice)	18 episodes
Vega$	Gloria Garland	Episode: "Love Affair"
The Ghosts of Buxley Hall	Ernestine Di Gonzini	Television film
Fantasy Island	Various roles	3 episodes
Elvis and the Beauty Queen	Su-Su	Television movie
The Smurfs	Additional voices	Unknown episodes

Title	Role	Notes
Three's Company	Marsha	Episode: "The Matchbreakers"
Simon & Simon	Penny Russell	Episode: "Matchmaker"
Madame's Place	Kaye Jacobs	Episode #1.42
CHiPs	Babe	Episode: "Journey to a Spacecraft"
The Rousters	Mrs. Slade	Episode: "Slade vs. Slade"
Hotel	Georgia Potter	Episode: "Ideals"
1st & Ten	Rona	4 episodes
The Love Boat	Harriet Wolters	1 episode
Benson	Zelda	Episode: "Solid Gold"
Scooby-Doo and the Ghoul School	Revolta (Voice)	Television movie
Coming of Age	Pauline Spencer	15 episodes
Sweet Bird of Youth	Sally Powers	Television movie
Jake and the Fatman	Leilani Simmons	Episode: "Sweet Leilani"
Timeless Tales from Hallmark	Voice role	Episode: "Rapunzel"
Charles in Charge	Gloria	Episode: "Three Dates and a Walnut"
People Like Us	Faye Converse	Television film
Murder, She Wrote	Renee	Episode: "A Body to Die For"
Delta	Charlotte Tyler	Episode: "How Much Is That Darden in the Window?"
The Building	Sylvia	Episode: "Yakkity Yak Don't Talk"
Roseanne	Joyce	2 episodes
Saved by the Bell: The New Class	Mrs. Gore	Episode: "Cigar Wars"
Power Rangers: Lightspeed Rescue	Koko Kashmere	Episode: "In the Limelight"

279

Title	Role	Notes
Life With Bonnie	Mrs. Ruta Blanchette	Episode: "Places, Stat!"
Studio House	Lily Fargate	Television movie
Christmas Do-Over	Granny Conlon	Television movie
Christmas at Cadillac Jack's	Rose Jenkins	Television movie
Days of Our Lives	Tillie Inman	Episode #1.11749
Seven Brides for Seven Brothers	Ruth	Credited as Ruta Kilmonis
The Girl in the Red Velvet Swing	Tennis Girl	Uncredited
The Twinkle in God's Eye	Ruthie	Movie
Anything Goes	Girl	Uncredited
Gaby	Denise	Movie
Funny Face	Lettie	Movie
Witness for the Prosecution	Diana	Movie
Marjorie Morningstar	Imogene Norman	Movie
Operation Eichmann	Anna Kemp	Movie
Sergeants 3	Amelia Parent	Movie
The Gun Hawk	Marleen	Movie
Hootenanny Hoot	A.G. Bannister	Movie
Bullet for a Badman	Lottie	Alternative title: *Renegade Posse*
Invisible Diplomats	Connie Wisner	Short subject produced by AT&T
Doomsday Machine	Dr. Marion Turner	Alternative title: *Escape from Planet Earth* ; shot in 1967
Rooster: Spurs of Death!	Gayly	Movie

Title	Role	Notes
Cracking Up	Ms. Sultry (voice)	Alternative title: *Smorgasbord* Movie
Funny Bones	Laura Fawkes	Movie
Pterodactyl Woman from Beverly Hills	Mrs. Poole	Movie
Pretty When You Cry	Antique Store Patron	Alternative title: *Seduced: Pretty When You Cry*
Quiet Kill	Doris	Alternative title: *Nightmare Boulevard*
Sadie and the Slot Machines	Sadie Silver	Short film
A Christmas Too Many	Grandma	Direct-to-DVD release
Forever Young at Heart	Shelley Felgerstein	Short film
For Better or for Worse		Movie

Ruta's Stage Credits as "Leading Lady"

- A Little Night Music
- Kiss Me Kate
- Annie Get Your Gun
- Lorelei
- Bells Are Ringing
- Mame

- Best Little Whore House in Texas
- On The Town
- Call Me Madam
- The Owl and the Pussycat
- 42nd Street
- Pajama Game
- Funny Girl
- Peter Pan
- Goodbye Charlie
- Peter Pat
- Guys and Dolls
- SameTime Next Year
- Gypsy
- Showboat
- Hello Dolly
- South Pacific
- Irene
- Sugarbabies
- Irma La Douce
- Grossingers
- Unsinkable Molly Brown
- Steel Magnolias
- A Little Night Music
- Hello Sucker
- Woman of the Year

Epilogue

It has been our privilege to work with Ruta Lee. Her book provides its readers with a fascinating insight into the golden years of Hollywood. Her memoirs are rich with tales of her stage performances and game shows all the while crossing paths with sparkling and famous personalities along the way.

Ruta's incredible career spans decades. Her historical career is told with truth and humor that are the trademarks of Ruta's exciting life. Ruta's journey highlights the fun she had along the way as she rose to the very top of her profession. We at Briton Publishing are honored to share these stories of movie history with a rare look behind the scenes.

Her stories are a precious insight into a world that most of us will never see. Thankfully, these stories will never be forgotten along with the priceless photos, each a split second in time, never to be repeated.

Thank you Ruta for sharing your beautiful life with all of us.

Much love,

Tony, Brinka and Rob

Briton Publishing LLC.